Sixteen Men

SIXTEEN MEN

*Understanding Masculine
Personality Types*

LOREN E. PEDERSEN, PH.D.

SHAMBHALA

Boston & London

1993

Shambhala Publications, Inc.
Horticultural Hall
300 Massachusetts Avenue
Boston, Massachusetts 02115

9 8 7 6 5 4 3 2 1

First Edition
Printed in the United States of America on acid-free
paper ♾

Distributed in the United States by Random House,
Inc., and in Canada by Random House of Canada Ltd

Library of Congress Cataloging-in-Publication Data
Pedersen, Loren E., 1941–
    Sixteen men: understanding masculine personality types/
Loren E. Pedersen.
      p.   cm.
    Includes bibliographical references and index.
    ISBN 0-87773-692-8 (pbk.)
    1. Men—Psychology. 2. Typology
(Psychology)   3. Typology (Psychology)
—Case studies.   4. Myers-Briggs Type Indicator.
I. Title. II. Title: 16 men.
BF692.5.P43 1993   92-56458
155.3'32—dc20   CIP

This book is dedicated to Hal Batt, Ph.D.

Contents

Acknowledgments

I would like to express my appreciation to the many patients, colleagues, and friends who have allowed me to use behavioral descriptions of their psychological type to create examples for this book. In doing so, they have added much substance and vitality to the sometimes static descriptions of the sixteen psychological types.

To my literary agent, Rosalie Siegel, for her continued trust and faith in the importance of my need to write about my clinical and personal experience.

To my editor (for the second time) Emily Hilburn Sell, who demonstrated and used the rare combination of both good thinking and warm feeling in editing my manuscript. She reaffirms the possibility that the relationship between editor and author can be productive, mutually educative, and most of all, enjoyable.

To Gerald P. Macdaid, of the Center for the Applications of Psychological Type, for his kindness in answering many research questions about psychological type and the Myers-Briggs Type Indicator.

To my friend and colleague, Frank R. Wilson, M.D., who over many late night dinners listened, supported, and advised me throughout the writing of *Sixteen Men*.

ACKNOWLEDGMENTS

To my friend and mentor for twenty years, Alexander J. Nemeth, Ph.D., for his warm, fatherly, and genteel wisdom.

To my friend, Eric Greenleaf, for his support, encouragement, and reading of the manuscript.

To John Beebe, M.D., for his encouragement and reading of the drafts of *Sixteen Men*.

To Joseph Henderson, M.D., for his presence, wisdom, and example.

To Joseph Wheelwright, M.D., one of the "granddaddies" of psychological type.

To my best, dearest, and oldest friend, Robert G. Lange, for twenty-five years of friendship, support, and conversation.

To Karen Diane, a female ESTJ, for her diligent and often last-minute efforts to fill in the gaps in my inferior extraverted thinking.

Introduction

UNDERSTANDING MEN THROUGH TYPOLOGY

In the past three decades we have witnessed a period of progressive concern for the social, political, and economic needs of women. Women themselves generated the energy for this interest. Their increasing success in separating from inflexible societal sex roles and redefining themselves has created the beginnings of a new awareness of women as individuals as well as a more distinct psychology of women.

More recently, an increasing number of books about men as well as a trend toward what might loosely be called a "men's movement" has led to a new interest in men. There is much grappling and confusion about the role of the "new man"—who he is, who he is supposed to be, and the basis for his psychology.

The media has given mixed—if not disparaging—attention to the emergence of men's interest in themselves by focusing on such ideas as Robert Bly's "wild man." The emphasis on primitive masculinity has at times created a caricature of a new male amounting to a parody of men's attempts to rediscover and redefine themselves. Cynical newspaper accounts of men gathering to "bump heads," wrestle, and endorse permissible flatulence have done little to further the ground of male psychology—for the observer, or for the participant.

In my previous book, *Dark Hearts: The Unconscious Forces That Shape Men's Lives,* I attempted to deepen our understanding of men by exploring the evolutionary, mythological, and psychological dimensions of their experience. I placed special emphasis on C. G. Jung's helpful idea of the *anima,* which consists of feminine representations of a man's unconscious found in his dreams, fantasies, and in projections onto actual women. My hope was that this would be a viable contribution to the emergence of a distinct, objective male psychology.

The present book, *Sixteen Men,* will supplement *Dark Hearts* through an objective approach derived from Jung's theory of psychological types, which is a valuable resource for men's clinical work and personal growth. The theory surrounding types is a source of stimulating ideas regarding male psychology and simultaneously an intriguing method of viewing the processes of consciousness as well as some lesser developed aspects of personality.

Sixteen Men also enhances the understanding of men's personalities by drawing on the extensive data from the research generated from the Myers-Briggs Type Indicator (MBTI), which has extended and clarified Jung's original thinking. In addition, it draws on my own extensive clinical use of the MBTI as a Jungian analyst working with men. In writing this book I have also tried to read all of the existing literature on psychological type, whether or not I thought it was relevant, or pertinent to my point of view. I have tried to incorporate as much of it as possible.

Type theory offers a fairly objective means of evaluating and using men's personality differences as they are reflected in their psychological type—not only the differences between men, but also between men and women. I am especially intrigued by the clear correlation between men's preference for the thinking process and women's preference for the feeling process. The overwhelming dominance of the thinking process in men might reflect a psychological preference that explains much of the difference between the behavior and attitudes of men and women. This cardinal difference may be interpreted, as it often is, as an innate, psychologically manifested sex difference. Or, it may reflect gender-based sex roles that are largely the outcome of differences in socialization. Either of these interpretations, or both, may be seen as having evolved out of the different biological, social, and psychological demands made on each of the sexes in the course of their evolution. In either or both cases, these differences may help us to better understand some of men's behavior and attitudes.

The preference for thinking over feeling in itself provides a source for a number of stimulating ideas regarding differences between male and female psychology. Whether this difference is truly innate remains to be seen.

TYPOLOGY: A STRUCTURAL *AND* DYNAMIC MODEL

As a model, typology provides both a structural and dynamic approach to understanding the various components of consciousness. Typology provides a framework or system for viewing aspects of personality that appear to cluster in patterns. It is an objective means for observing the different ways in which individuals both perceive and evaluate their life experiences as well as their sense of inner and outer reality.

Typology informs us that the motivations, values, and interests of individuals within one type group are likely to be somewhat consistent, and simultaneously, are likely to be different from those of other type groups. Knowing our own type and the type of others allows us to understand how to accept our differences as well as our similarities. For example, some conflicts arise simply from the different ways individuals approach and respond to their life experience, rather than from specific contents of real disagreements. As a structural approach, typology provides descriptive categories for the relative dominance of the primary *functions* of consciousness, that is of thinking, feeling, sensation, and intuition. It also gives the "attitude" of the type, which is either extraverted or introverted. And last, it identifies the preference of the individual for either a "judging" or "perceiving" orientation to the outer world. We will return to these structural elements in more detail in the first chapter.

Jungian typology is not an absolute system that narrowly locks individuals into rigid categories. Though individuals may be of the same type, the degree to which they are "true" to a particular type also varies. And, of course, specific individual differences unrelated to type also remain distinct. There is no such thing as a "pure" type. There is room for significant variability even within individual type profiles. All of us have some of the characteristics of each of the type elements as well as characteristics of each type profile. Also, different life histories, life experiences, and varieties of emotional and intellectual makeup create broad diversity between individuals, even of the same type. In addition to that, specific archetypal constellations may play a role in characterizing the collective aspects of an individual within a type group.[1]

When a dynamic view is added to these very workable descriptions of individual types, typology then also offers a concrete model for a psychology of consciousness, and can do so without being needlessly complex. As a dynamic model, typology elucidates some of the major characteristics of the healthy personality. It is through coming to terms with the undeveloped parts of one's personality that the potential of the dynamic aspect of typology becomes most clear. Psychological strengths, as well as weaknesses, can be made more explicit by the individual type profile. This kind of specific assessment can help focus our direction toward new psychological, emotional, and ultimately, spiritual growth.

WHY WRITE ABOUT MEN AND TYPE?

The use of typology has grown in recent years with increasing applications in the fields of psychology, counseling, personality research, education, and career development, and concerning religious and spiritual issues. The Center for the Applications of Psychological Type (CAPT) promotes books on psychological type and sponsors national workshops on the applications, theory, and research of psychological type. Jungian typology appeals to our rather universal desire to know more about ourselves. It provides an objective context for perceiving and evaluating our preferred psychological processes, which allows us to see ourselves, our relationships, work choices, and even personal values more clearly. It also offers a specific and practical framework for looking at categories of attitudes and behavior while preserving the integrity of individual differences.

This book is one of the first to be published about men and psychological type. The specific value of writing about the typology of men is that it provides a unique frame of reference for looking at men's behavior and attitudes as they are expressed by specific styles of perceiving and judging personal experience. Men's behavior can then be seen as a more predictable outcome of these various styles. This view of men is further enhanced by examining how they may differ typologically from women, and what the consequences are of these different type combinations in relationship.

HOW TO USE THIS BOOK

In the first chapter, I describe the structural elements of psychological type and the ways in which they combine to make each of the sixteen individual type profiles. This is the "nuts and bolts" of typology and is essential to understanding the rest of the book.

In the second chapter, I discuss how psychological type is relevant to the communication and relational styles men use in their everyday interactions with others. Typology is helpful in understanding not only the content of communication, but also the impact different communication styles may have on the listener. I also offer a critique of the popular idea that communication styles are a function of sex differences, and relate them instead to the combined effect of psychological type and sex-role socialization.

In the four central chapters, I present the sixteen psychological types by dividing them into four groups of four individual types, personified by fictional male characters. These groups are divided on the basis of sharing a common nucleus, consisting of a particular perceiving function with a particular judging function. These profiles were written with the intention of emphasizing both the natural strengths and weaknesses of the various types created by the interactive effect of various components of type. In each of these chapters, I have broken down the types into both vignettes and prototypes. The vignettes are personifications of the different types, clothed in the character of individuals I have actually known either as patients or friends. The prototypes attempt to describe the overriding characteristics of each type as they might occur within any individual.

By using these divisions as an overview, readers will be able to develop a general orientation to psychological type through seeing some of the potential behavioral effects of the various combinations of type elements. They will then be able to find some objective ways of looking at their own personalities by comparing traits of their own with the psychological characteristics found in both the vignettes and the prototypes of the sixteen types. If readers are moved to further explore themselves in terms of psychological type, they may wish to take the Myers-Briggs Type Indicator through a psychologist or psychiatrist who administers it. A self-administered test is also found in *Please Understand Me* by David Keirsey and Marilyn Bates.

OCCUPATION AND TYPE

Another practical area of interest enhanced by a knowledge of typology is the relationship between occupational choice and psychological type. There has been an increasing interest in recent years in finding more specific and dependable ways to evaluate the "fit" between individual types and specific career interests.

There is a wealth of research information presently available on type and career choice. Typological theory addresses the attraction to, and aptitude for, particular occupations and the likelihood that one possesses or can develop specific skills needed for them. Specific psychological types are overwhelmingly represented in certain professions and underrepresented in others, irrespective of the frequency of the type in the general population. Because of this, typology is a valuable occupational tool that can be used to help individuals decide whether their choice of profession is suited to their particular temperament. At the end of each prototype, I have included some of the frequent occupations of that type.

Appropriate matching of occupation and type can lead to increased employee satisfaction and less "burnout." It can also aid employers in refining recruitment procedures to select the appropriate individuals best matched to or suited for specific positions and advancements. There is a high correlation between the nucleus of a type group to specific occupational interest and categories of occupations. For example, some years ago the Gray-Wheelwright Type Inventory was used to assess Jungian analysts in California. That study found that 90 percent of analysts were introverted and 86 percent were intuitive.[2] What is remarkable about this finding is that the introverted intuitive types represent an extremely small fraction of the entire type population (about 5 percent).

THERAPEUTIC USES OF TYPOLOGY

A knowledge of typology is extremely useful in conflict mediation for couples, families, and even employer-employee relations. The application of Jung's theory of psychological types, specifically to the psychology of men, can be a valuable resource for men interested in their personal growth. It can also help therapists make their clinical work with men more understandable and productive.

Sharing the ideas of typology with men in therapy can create a balancing, objective context in which they may better understand more of their personal dynamics and personality development.

Understanding and using differences and similarities between the therapist's and patient's psychological type can increase the quality of rapport between them. It can also influence the course of treatment by making issues like transference and countertransference more understandable, and in some cases even more predictable.

Typology gives the therapist a valuable diagnostic tool. It also provides a model for a healthy psychology of consciousness. As such, it offers a means of looking at individual strengths as well as areas of personality needing further development. In this way, both the structural and dynamic aspects of type can be used directly.

THE GOAL OF *SIXTEEN MEN*

A thorough knowledge of both the positive and negative attributes of each type provides concrete guidelines for continuing to develop one's strengths as well as for improving those areas of personality in need of development and change.

All of the aspects of masculine psychology, described here in typological terms, will hopefully help both men and women achieve a deeper understanding of the strengths and weaknesses, and the advantages and disadvantages of men's personalities, as well as an understanding of how men communicate.

My goal here, as it was in *Dark Hearts,* is to help men deepen their appreciation of their personalities and provide a little more light on their paths of self-discovery. It would also be especially, personally fulfilling to me if *Sixteen Men* enhanced women's feeling for what it is like to be a man.

Perhaps the most important reason to use typology is that it is very practical. Typology works well as a creative tool in understanding relationships between men and their partners, children, and friends. I hope that *Sixteen Men* will be a welcome and worthwhile contribution to what seems to be a growing literature on the psychology of men.

CHAPTER 1

What Is Typology?

In every psychology of the future, the chapter devoted to psychological types will be an increasingly important one. Between the individual and the species stands the type. The plan of personality is neither a standardized repetition of a uniform unit, nor a haphazard medley or mosaic; there runs through its designs a limited set of groupings.
    —J. Jastrow

BACKGROUND

When Jung's book *Psychological Types* was finally published in 1920, it was the culmination of nearly twenty years of clinical work. Its inception also followed closely on Jung's break with Freud following the Fourth Psychoanalytic Congress in Munich in 1912. Jung described the interval following this break as his "fallow period," which lasted from 1913 to 1917 or 1918. It was a time of deep introspection characterized by his attempts to understand troubling images that sprung from his unconscious.

This prolonged period of self-examination, his recovery from his disrupted relationship with Freud, and the ensuing years of his clinical practice resulted in what is perhaps Jung's most articulate exposition of conscious processes. It was essential that he understand these processes in preparation for exploring the unconscious. Jung's theory of psychological types is one of the great contributions to our understanding of mental processes and thus of important aspects of human behavior. In an editorial note, Jung states:

> My book, therefore, was an effort to deal with the relationship of the individual to the world, to people and things. It discussed the various aspects of consciousness, the various attitudes the conscious mind might take toward the world, and thus constitutes *a psychology of consciousness* regarded from what might be called a clinical angle.[1]

JUNG'S TYPOLOGY AS A PSYCHOLOGY OF CONSCIOUSNESS

As a theory, typology describes the primary functions of consciousness and how individuals use them differently. Typology is one approach to the psychology of consciousness that uses a model of sixteen different possible ways of perceiving, judging, and behaving. As an infrastructure it conceptualizes much of how consciousness "works." As a psychology of consciousness, typology basically describes how we perceive and the judgments we make about those perceptions. When we understand typology, the workings of our mental processes become more familiar, more understandable, and even more predictable. Much of our behavior can be understood as the outcome of the various ways we use our type. Once we understand this, a good deal of the mystery about ourselves and others becomes less baffling.

Typology helps us understand consciousness as a relatively predictable outcome of specific ways of perceiving and judging our experience. The apparent mechanical quality of type function may seem simplistic, and to an extent it is. For instance, conscious processes do not occur so discretely and separately that we can label them as they occur. Our perceptions, for example, are not always "awake." We can register a perception and not know we perceived it.

The same is true of another component of consciousness reflected in typology: judgment. Human beings are never neutral, even when they appear to be. All that we perceive is either somehow "good or bad," liked or disliked, makes sense or is nonsense, with lots of shades of in-between. In any case, none of our judgments are neutral. Like our perceptions, our judgments are not always "awake." For example, just as we can register a perception and not know we perceived it, we also can make a judgment and not know we made it. In either case, whether or not we are aware of either the perception or the judgment, we may be made aware of our perceptions and our judgments by their effects. We call these effects our behavior.

So, all behavior is the effect, or outcome, of both a perception and a judgment, or even several of each. It can be discrete, brief—gone even before it is observed. Its form may be a movement, an attitude, or even a physiological reaction. Or it can be a complex series of interconnected experiences, congealing into how we spend an hour, a day, or most of our lives. The importance of behavior has much to do with how influenced or determined we are by it versus how much of a conscious role we can assume in determining how we behave. Typology allows a means of evaluating conscious behavior by examining "what" we perceive and the judgments that accompany those perceptions.

HOW JUNG DERIVED THE COMPONENTS OF TYPOLOGY

On an objective level, typology was Jung's description of the dominant process of consciousness. On a subjective level, he derived *Psychological Types* largely from his attempt to deal with his own "psychological particularity," as well as the outcome of his "personal dealings with friend and with foe." A particularly personal focus was on his relationship with Freud and the dissension that erupted in Freud's early circle of followers.[2] Realizing the limits of objectivity in his struggle with Freud, he decided to examine the conflict between Freud and Alfred Adler, another of Freud's early disciples. His analysis of the struggle between Freud and Adler led him to the idea of introversion and extraversion. He saw the differences between them as resulting from Freud's extraverted approach compared to Adler's introverted approach. He writes:

> The Freud-Adler controversy is simply a paradigm and one single instance among many possible attitude-types. . . . The first attitude [introversion] is normally characterized by a hesitant, reflective, retiring nature that keeps itself to itself, shrinks from objects, is always slightly on the defensive and prefers to hide behind mistrustful scrutiny. The second [extraversion] is normally characterized by an outgoing, candid, and accommodating nature that adapts easily to a given situation, quickly forms attachments, and, setting aside any possible misgivings, will often venture forth with careless confidence into unknown situations. In the first case obviously the subject, and in the second the object, is all-important.[3]

INTROVERSION AND EXTRAVERSION

These personal orientations to the outer versus the inner world described by Jung later became the "attitudes" of the Myers-Briggs Type Indicator. Isabel Briggs Myers described them as a preference for focusing one's attention. According to her, extraverts preferred "to focus on the outer world of people and the external environment. So, extraversion is a preference primarily directed to the outer world, focusing on people and objects. When you are extraverting, you become *energized* by what goes on in the outer world, so this is where you tend to direct your energy. Extraverts usually prefer to communicate more by talking than by writing. They need to experience the world to understand it and thus usually like action."

Introverts, on the other hand, are people who prefer to focus on their inner world. Introversion directs itself to the inner world, focusing on concepts and ideas. "When you are introverting, you are *energized* by what goes on in your inner world, and so this is where you tend to direct your energy. Introverts tend to be more interested and comfortable when their work requires a good deal of their activity to take place quietly inside their heads. They like to understand the world before experiencing it, and so often think about what they are doing before acting." The essential difference between extraverts and introverts shows up as the "action orientation" of the extravert and the "reflective orientation" of the introvert.[4]

According to Jung, these attitudes show the dominant direction in which an individual's psychic energy moves. Because of this, introverts and extraverts behave very differently and will often have a difficult time understanding each other, even if other aspects of their type are the same or similar.

As we will see, there are advantages and disadvantages to

each orientation depending on the requirements of the specific situations in which individuals find themselves.

THE FUNCTIONS OF CONSCIOUSNESS

Jung understood that the concepts of introversion and extraversion helped one understand significant differences in points of view. In addition, he isolated other dimensions of conscious experience that are called "functions." These functions show the way in which individuals perceive and judge their experience. In his early formulations Jung pointed out that these functions describe the way in which the ego, as the center of consciousness, relates and orients itself to information coming into its sphere from outside of it. He called these processes the *ectopsychic* facts of consciousness. These were distinguished from the *endopsychic* facts that pertained to "a system of relationship between the contents of consciousness and postulated processes in the unconscious."[5]

All the various functions arise from an originally unconscious state and find their way into consciousness only gradually. Since the functions arise in a developmental way, the primary or "dominant" function is the one most likely to become conscious first. For this reason it is the most available to consciousness. We sometimes see this in children when their dominant mode of consciousness becomes obvious early in life.

All the functions are potentially available to consciousness and can be of service to the ego as tools in our attempts to understand and relate to others and to the world. How available the functions are to the ego determines the extent to which they are used, as in the old saying, "If all you have is a hammer, you're going to treat everything like a nail." The expression of each function can be either adaptive or maladaptive depending upon how rigidly or flexibly it is used and relied upon. The ideal, of course, would be that throughout our psychological growth we develop aspects of all of the functions. But, as we shall see, this is easier said than done.

SENSATION AND INTUITION: THE PERCEIVING FUNCTIONS

The first function Jung describes is *sensation,* "the sum total of my awareness of external facts given to me through the function of my senses. Sensation tells me that something *is:* it does not tell me *what* it is and it does not tell me other things about that something; it only tells me that something is."⁶ Myers describes sensing as the means of acquiring information from the senses to assess what is actually there both from the inside of the person as well as from the outside. She describes it as a means of "appreciating the realities of a situation." Individuals who rely on their senses "tend to accept and work with what is 'given' in the here and now, and thus become realistic and practical. They are good with working with a great number of facts."⁷ Sensation also imparts practicality and concreteness.

For Jung, *intuition* introduces the element of time. "Things have a past and they have a future. They come from somewhere, they go to somewhere, and you cannot see where they came from and you cannot know where they go to, but you get what the Americans call a hunch." Jung refers to intuition as "a sort of divination, a sort of miraculous faculty" that was essentially mysterious and "by which you see around corners, which you really cannot do. . . ."⁸ According to Myers, intuition is the other means of acquiring information that shows us the "meanings, relationships, and possibilities that go beyond the information from your senses. Intuition looks

at the bigger picture and tries to grasp the essential patterns."⁹
Intuition allows for the perception of new possibilities and
new ways of doing things. Unlike sensation, it is not a practical or concrete mode of perception.

Jung considers the perceiving functions of intuition and
sensation to be the *irrational* functions. This is because as
perceptual processes they have no direct relationship to the
reasoning process as such. Intuition is the more abstract perceiving function, involving meanings, relationships, and possibilities. Often the intuitive person operates by "hunches."
Hunches are often difficult to justify in objective terms, but to
the intuitive they feel very certain.

Sensation, on the other hand, is more concrete, involving
facts or occurrences perceived through one or more of the five
senses. At least sensation appears to have a more reliable, objective basis simply because the physical properties it detects
have a higher level of objectivity. Perceptions based on sensation also have a higher likelihood of consensual validation
since they employ the senses. Intuition, on the other hand,
seems to operate as if there were no consensual basis for its
reality, and hence is often considered an inferior mode of perception. One wonders whether this devaluation is partially
responsible for the relatively lesser numbers of intuitive types
among both men and women. Seventy percent of the population prefers the sensation mode of perception compared to
only 30 percent who prefer intuition.

Within the history of psychology as well as in science, the
study of perception has favored sensation over intuition as the
accepted mode of perception. The masculine bias inherent in
this emphasis grew out of traditional scientific reliance on the
measurable physical properties of matter registered by the
senses. Very early on, perceptual psychologists tried to
ground perception in a sensate reality because the properties

of sensation were, at least superficially, more readily quantifiable. Meanwhile, intuitive perceptions based on nonmeasurable qualities were largely ignored as legitimate matter to study.[10]

Yet even the supposedly "objective" basis for perception via the senses is questionable if one looks more deeply at the actual processes of perception. A closer look often reveals not only that the traditional view of perception is simplistic but also that the nature of perception itself is an enigma. We now know that perceptual processes are not the simple result of passive registration of sensation by sense organs, but rather a series of highly complex processes arising within the brain itself. They are influenced by early learning experiences, culture, memory, personal bias, and the psychology of the individual as well. Even illusions, for which any theory of perception must account, are not necessarily what they seem. What is clearly an illusion in one culture is not perceived as such in another. For example, the New Guinea tribespeople of the Torres Strait area don't perceive the illusion in the Müller-Lyer effect, comparing >—< with <—>. The tribespeople see the lines as of equal length. English-speaking people of the civilized world virtually always see the first line as longer than the second. The tribespeople's perception is influenced by not living in a world conditioned by objects that frequently display straight lines. In the modern world illusions are created by the fact that right angles can be seen in almost all intersections. Not so with the tribespeople—they may go their whole lives seeing but a few right angles.

Perhaps the difference between sensation and intuition as perceptual processes in typology is that sensation types seem to use outer stimuli or the environment more concretely than intuitives do. This may be somewhat analogous to the way extraverts are stimulated by the outer world and introverts use stimuli coming from their less obvious inner world. In the same way that our culture automatically gives greater consensual validation for sensation it also does for extraversion. As with sensation, 70 percent of the population is extraverted and only 30 percent introverted. Our society gives the greatest consensual validity to extraverted sensation as a mode of perceiving. This combination occurs in the population over five times more than introverted intuition in women and three times more than introverted intuition in men.

The presumed "truth" of sensate perceptions may not be more valid or more real than intuitive perceptions, but may merely appear so because the external environment can be cited as the evident basis or "cause" for the perception. Intuitive perception may be less reliant on the environment as such, perhaps even appearing to bypass it, and yet it is still a valid mode of perception. The distrust of intuition and its reliance on internal stimuli may be largely due to the lack of obvious physical determinants, as well as an even greater lack of physical principles to explain its operations.

THINKING AND FEELING: THE EVALUATIVE FUNCTIONS

The next function Jung describes is *thinking,* which in its simplest form tells *what* a thing is. "It gives a name to the thing."[11] Myers describes the thinking function as a means of making decisions by predicting "the logical consequences of any particular choice or action. When you use thinking you decide objectively, based on cause and effect, and make decisions by analyzing and weighing the evidence, even including the unpleasant facts. (Thinking seeks an) objective standard of truth (and thinkers) are frequently good at analyzing what is wrong with something."[12]

The last function is *feeling*. "Feeling informs you through its feeling-tones of the *values* of things. Feeling tells you for instance whether a thing is acceptable or agreeable or not. It tells you what a thing is worth to you."[13] Myers states, "Feeling considers what is important to you or to other people (without requiring that it be logical) and decides from person-centered values. Feeling types like being with and working with people and tend to become sympathetic, appreciative, and tactful."[14] Feeling does not refer to the conventional meaning of being emotional as such, but of making decisions based on values.

Together, thinking and feeling are called the judging functions because they involve judgments *about* the perceptions one has. Here, feeling does not involve emotionality per se (although emotionality is probably more often observed in individuals with extraverted feeling). The "feeling" person makes decisions or evaluations based on personal or social values, whereas the "thinking" person makes decisions in a more impersonal way, based on impersonal logical consequences. Jung considers thinking and feeling to both be *rational* functions "because both are based on a reflective, linear process that coalesces into a particular judgment."[15]

THE FOURFOLD STRUCTURE OF CONSCIOUSNESS

In any of us, one of these functions along with the attitude of either introversion or extraversion is ordinarily dominant. This dominance imparts a particular psychological character to us as individuals. Jung portrayed these four functions as represented by a quaternity in which the axes of the thinking-feeling continuum and the sensation-intuition continuum crossed in the center. The ego is at the center, with a certain amount of energy of willpower or intentionality at its disposal for the various functions.

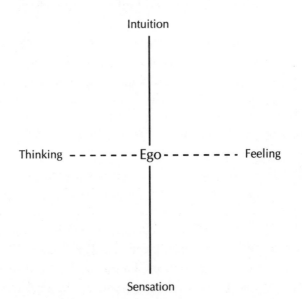

The dominance of one function often results in the lack of differentiation of the corresponding function at the other end of the continuum. For example, if thinking is dominant or more conscious, then feeling would usually be the less conscious. We call the least developed aspect the *inferior function.*

The following diagram illustrates this emphasis in a person who is a thinking type. In this case, thinking is shown as closer to the ego because it is dominant, and feeling is shown as relatively distant because it is least developed. Also in this case, intuition and sensation serve as auxiliary functions to the primary one.

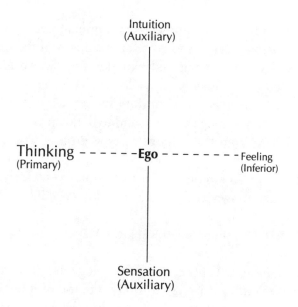

Years after Jung developed his theory of psychological type, research conducted by others further enhanced his original contribution. Horace Gray and Joseph Wheelwright developed the Gray-Wheelwright Type Indicator that was used for many years by Jungian analysts to type their analysands. The Gray-Wheelwright, the most frequently used inventory in the past, is now largely replaced by the Myers-Briggs Type Indicator (the MBTI), which the mother-daughter team of Katherine Briggs and Isabel Briggs Myers developed. The MBTI not only assesses one's individual typology but shows the relative degree to which each component contributes to the total type. The degree of extraversion, for example, may vary between individuals from slight to extreme.

In the last thirty years or so the MBTI has become the major source of typological research. It has been used to explore individual psychological development, occupations, personal preferences, personal relationships, and the various ways we have of viewing and experiencing the world. The Center for Applications of Psychological Type was organized as a service and research laboratory in 1975. It continues to conduct research using the MBTI, and to build an ever-increasing data base from the millions of type profiles scored each year.

There is also a more recent though not yet widely standardized test known as the Singer-Loomis Type Inventory.

J AND P: THE LIFESTYLE PREFERENCE

So, the main ingredients of Jung's typology are: introversion or extraversion, called one's *attitude;* the use of intuition or sensation as the mode of *perceiving;* and the use of thinking or feeling as the mode for *judging* those perceptions. Isabel Briggs Myers later added *lifestyle preference* to these others, making Jung's implicit ideas of perception and judgment more explicit.

Lifestyle preference, or the JP attitude, describes how an individual attempts to deal with the outer world—the manner he adopts in trying to deal with it. This outer world adaptation can be primarily through either a judging attitude (J = thinking or feeling) or a perceptive attitude (P = intuition or sensation) to observe the world.

So, the person who is *judging* likes to live in a more structured, planned, controlled, organized, and decision-directed manner. He does not like "loose ends," but likes things to be brought quickly to a conclusion through decisions, or "judgments." So, he uses a judgment function to seek closure or to decide on the appropriate action for his perception. One might say he reaches conclusions primarily through thinking or feeling. On the other hand, someone who has a *perceiving* disposition prefers an easy flow of events and enjoys flexibility and openness to the new, novel, spontaneous, and unexpected. This person will likely not need to make decisions as quickly as their judging counterpart, but will be more tolerant of ambiguity. He perceives the world by using a perceptive function, sensing or intuiting to observe or take in the situation.

Like dominant handedness, where we use both hands, but have come to trust, develop, and therefore prefer to use one hand over the other, our type profile indicates our preferences or propensities rather than an absolute way of being. All of us use some introversion and some extraversion as well as each of the functions to some extent.

DEGREES OF TYPE PREFERENCE

Not all of us use each of the components of type to the same degree. So assigning a particular type is always a matter of propensity and degree of use. Because of this, some of us are "truer" to a particular type designation than others. On the Myers-Briggs Type Indicator the components of type are broken down according to the degree to which particular individuals express the various components of their type.

For example, there are extreme introverts, or those whose scores indicate they prefer introversion almost to the exclusion of extraversion. For them, whatever can be said of introverts will not only apply, but will seem to hit the mark much more so than someone who scores in the middle range.

Then there are some individuals who score toward the middle of the scale on one or more of the components. For example, someone scoring in the middle of the introversion-extraversion scale might be considered an "ambivert." Scoring as an ambivert may result from having developed introversion and extraversion equally, or it may result from a lack of differentiation between the two. In other words, ambiverts may either have equal access to introverted and extraverted propensities, or they may be confused about which they prefer.

A lack of differentiation between functions may also result from early life experience in which parents reinforce one or more components of type that are not natural for their children. For example, two extremely extraverted parents who have an introverted child may reinforce extraverted behavior, and downplay, or even punish, introverted behavior. Without an understanding of typology, these parents may even perceive the introverted child as pathologically shy or withdrawn.

If too many of the natural components of the child's type are negatively reinforced, a "turntype" may result. Turntypes are individuals who behave as if they are a type that they are not. This can occur with respect to one component or all of the components of type.

COMBINING THE INGREDIENTS

Each type profile creates a shorthand description of these eight possibilities, which are represented by initialized letters. Each letter stands for the function it represents. The exception is intuition, which is represented by the letter N, to distinguish it from introversion. So, we have:

I for introversion	T for thinking
E for extraversion	F for feeling
N for intuition	J for judging
S for sensation	P for perceiving

Any individual type profile has one of each of these paired possibilities. Thus, the type profile represents a four-letter combination describing the person's preferred attitude (I or E), preferred mode of perceiving (N or S), preferred mode of judging (T or F), and preferred lifestyle preference (P or J). The various possible combinations of these ingredients result in a total of sixteen four-letter combinations, or types:

ESTJ	ESFJ	ENTJ	ENFJ
ESTP	ESFP	ENTP	ENFP
ISTJ	ISFJ	INTJ	INFJ
ISTP	ISFP	INTP	INFP

Thus we have the sixteen (letter designated) types representing the attitudes and functions most conscious or available to an individual designated by that type. Anyone who develops a sufficient familiarity with typology will find himself or herself more or less accurately represented by one of these sixteen types.

HOW TYPE WORKS

Individuals can usually be understood better through descriptions of their personality types, which indicate what they are likely to do best. Inferences about their psychological type could also be made by observing what they have the most difficult time doing. They could also be classified by looking at their "shadow types"—other types that embody their least developed, or inferior, functions. Each type is likely to have some distinct strengths as well as specific weaknesses. None is perfect, and none is "better"; they are simply different.

Although the elements of typology are presented in a somewhat hierarchical format, in real life it is not all that neat. Among all of the types there are individuals who have not succeeded in developing or differentiating any aspect of their typological makeup. These are often low-functioning individuals who are not likely to have made an adequate adaptation to others or to the world. Then there are others who, by dint of a great deal of inner psychological and emotional work, have been successful in developing most of their psychological functions. By maximizing the greatest potential of most of their functions these types have succeeded in achieving healthy, productive lives. Jung called this process "individuation." The goal of individuation is not only to develop as much of oneself as one can, but to become all that one's unique individuality has to offer.

SEX OR GENDER DIFFERENCES IN TYPOLOGY

In meeting and working with all sixteen types represented in this book, I have been struck by the fact that these sixteen possible types are far from equally distributed within a sample population of men. This is also true, although in a different way, of the occurrence of types in the population of women. For example, 61 percent of men use the thinking function, while 68 percent of women use the feeling function. This thinking-feeling polarity is an essential and important difference between men and women from the typological standpoint. (For more information on this, see tables 1 through 6 in the appendix.)

These differences between men and women are a fertile area for both psychological speculation and future research. For example, not only are there differences between the sexes with respect to thinking and feeling, there is a disproportionately large number of thinking type men within the male group itself. The most common male type, extraverted thinking, occurs nearly *seventeen* times more frequently than the least common male type, introverted intuition. It becomes immediately obvious from this that there is great variability in type distribution even among men.

To get a general overview of the types of men and women and their type frequency in the American population, try to visualize a gathering of one hundred men. Imagine that the various personality types of all males are present in proportion to their frequency in the general population. The group probably would be quite boisterous since there will be three times as many extraverts as introverts. About sixty of these men would value their thinking processes over feeling processes. Forty-one of them would have a nucleus of ST in their type. Twenty more of them would have a nucleus of NT in their type. Twenty-five would have SF as the nucleus of their type. And the remainder of men, only thirteen, would have NF as the nucleus of theirs. You would also observe that their occupations were highly correlated with the nucleus of their personality type.

On the other hand, a group of women representing their occurrence by type would be composed quite differently. Only twenty-three women would be STs; forty-seven women would be SFs; only nine would be NTs; and twenty women would be NFs.

Comparing men and women with respect to distribution by type, we can see that there is either a strong genetic or gender bias in typology. This bias results in a major difference between men and women; that is, well over 60 percent of men have thinking as a strong component in their type, and well over 60 percent of women have feeling as a strong component in their type.

This thinking or feeling component in combination with a perceiving function (s or n) forms the nucleus of a man or woman's type. The combination of either of the perceiving functions with either of the judging functions results in four nuclei. The nucleus of each type manifests in a unique interactive behavioral effect. The main chapters of this book are organized in a way that emphasizes each type's nucleus, and built around this core are other nongender, non-sex-linked components that further fill out or embellish the individual character.

To elaborate on this point, the sensation (S) function is gender-neutral and occurs equally in men and women in 70 percent of the population. So in men, the thinking component is most frequently associated with sensation (ST), and likewise, sensation occurs most often with feeling in women (SF). For example, the fact that there are twice as many women as men in the sensation-feeling group also helps explain why traditionally more women are found in the "helping professions." Extraversion is likewise gender-neutral and also occurs in 70 percent of the population. Introversion, again, is gender-neutral and occurs in only 30 percent of the population.

What is so important here is that the behavioral correlates of thinking or feeling processes often create the misperception of sex differences rather than differences derived from type. What typologically is most "masculine" is extraverted thinking-sensation, and what is typologically most "feminine" is extraverted feeling-sensation. It is probably closer to the truth to say that the thinking-feeling polarity is first and foremost a difference in typology, not a true sex difference.

In spite of the fact that certain types occur more frequently in males or females, it is presumptuous and erroneous to connect these type differences only to the respective sexes. Women who are extraverted thinking sensation types may be as psychologically "masculine" as men of that type, and men who are extraverted feeling sensation types may be as "feminine" as women of that type. If we accept this, we are then free to speculate about a more intriguing issue: why do typological characteristics occur as they do in the respective sexes?

In this light, conventional notions of masculinity and femininity as attributions of sex become much more relative, or context bound, than has been assumed. Further, the issue of whether a given man or woman is allowed the social freedom to express the full ramifications of their typological makeup is even more complex.

In spite of these highly significant differences, there has been little research exploring the specific reasons for such a divergence between men and women. While most writers and researchers of typology presume the type of the individual to be innate, the imbalanced distribution of types raises some interesting questions about "innateness." Whether type is innate or not, understanding this thinking-feeling polarity may amount to a significant contribution in understanding male-female differences.

DETERMINING THE DOMINANT FUNCTION

Each of the sixteen types is described by a ranking of functions. We all have some capacity to express each function, but its expression depends on how much we use it. That is, its expression depends on its availability to consciousness. Each of us has a *dominant* function, an *auxiliary* function, a *tertiary* function, and an *inferior* function.

The dominant function is simply what one does most of the time. Extraverts and introverts use it differently. Extraverts use their dominant function in the outer world, since that's "where they are" most of the time. Introverts use the dominant function in the inner world, since that is where they spend most of their time. This difference between introverts and extraverts has important behavioral consequences, since both have to deal with the outer world whether they prefer to or not. We will return to this later.

What any of us "do most" is determined partly by whether we are introverts or extraverts as well as by our outer world preference, J or P. For extraverts, we arrive at this in the following way: Ted, for example, is an extravert whose type profile is designated by the letter combination of ESTJ. The E at the beginning of the profile tells us this person is an extravert, but it doesn't automatically tell us *which* of the functions of his profile, S (sensation) or T (thinking), he uses most of the time. To figure out Ted's dominant function we need to know whether his outer world orientation is judging, J, or perceiving, P. The letter J at the end tells us that Ted's orientation to the outer world is through judging. What this means is that what Ted "does most" will be expressed through either thinking or feeling, since those are the judging functions. Ted prefers thinking over feeling—he is an ESTJ. Therefore, we say that Ted's dominant function is extraverted thinking.

On the other hand, for an extravert like Jake (ESTP), who has P at the end of the profile, the dominant function is determined a little differently. He too is an extravert, but since P occurs at the end of his profile rather than J, we know that Jake uses perceiving as his way of orienting to the outer world. So in Jake's case, as with other extraverts having P at the end of the profile, the dominant function must be either intuition or sensation, since those are the perceiving functions. Since sensation is part of the nucleus of Jake's profile, we say that Jake is an extraverted sensation type.

The J or P functions also decide the dominant function for introverts, but in a slightly different way than for extraverts. J and P have more to do with relating to the outer world, and introverts spend more time relating to their inner world. Therefore, for introverts we derive the dominant function differently.

We can use Richard, an ISTJ, for this example. Looking at his profile we know that he is an introvert. J is at the end of his profile, *but* it refers to outer world orientation, and he does as little of that as possible. His dominant function is going to be determined by what he does most of the time. Therefore, Richard's dominant function will be introverted sensation rather than introverted thinking. Similarly, the introvert Harry, an ISTP, will have his dominant function determined by the lifestyle preference P and his introversion. His dominant function is introverted thinking.

Because Richard is an ISTJ, we call his dominant function introverted sensation. But introverted thinking is Harry's dominant function because he is an ISTP. Since they are both introverts, their outer world preference (J or P) is *secondary*. So for ISTJs, the dominant function will be the *opposite* of their preference for the outer world, in this case, perceiving. Therefore their dominant function will be introverted sensation. Likewise, the dominant function of ISTPs is the *opposite* of their outer world lifestyle preference, which in this case is judging. Therefore their dominant function will be introverted thinking.

DETERMINING THE AUXILIARY FUNCTIONS

Once we determine the dominant type, we want to know which function is likely to serve the second most important role. To what degree the secondary function is developed is an individual matter.

This secondary or auxiliary function can be derived simply by taking the introverted or extraverted attitude that is the opposite of the dominant function and adding the remaining function from the "core" of the four-letter designation. So for Ted, an ESTJ (extraverted thinking), introverted sensation is his secondary or auxiliary function.

The dominant function helps us determine the auxiliary functions. The auxiliary functions are theoretically the second and third most available to us. For example, as an extravert with thinking as his dominant function, Ted needs a secondary means of accessing his inner world. Ted's secondary access is less developed than his extraverted thinking. Because it is less available to him we call it his auxiliary function. In these examples the auxiliary functions would be introverted sensation for ESTJ and introverted intuition for ENTJ. In the case of the ESTP and ESFP, whose dominant functions are both extraverted sensation, the auxiliary functions would then be introverted thinking and introverted feeling.

In the case of Richard, the ISTJ, we determine his auxiliary function by noting that since he is a judging type, his thinking goes toward the outer world. And since he is an introvert, his outer world orientation will be his auxiliary function, extraverted thinking. In Harry's case, the ISTP, the auxiliary function is determined by the fact that he is a perceiving type. And because he is also an introvert, his outer world orientation will also be his auxiliary function, extraverted sensation.

When one of these secondary functions is well developed, it gives the introvert or extravert a measure of balance between his inner and outer world. That is, an extraverted thinker like Ted can gain some access to his inner world through introverted sensation. And an introverted sensation type like Richard gains access to the outer world through extraverted thinking.

So, the importance of the auxiliary function for any type is to supply balance between the lifestyle preferences of perception and judgment, and the attitudes of introversion and extraversion.[16]

In general, the extraverts' dominant function is more obvious to others than their auxiliary. Extraverts are naturally already "in the world," spending most of their time and energy there, and they relate to it primarily with their dominant function. With them, it is more a case of "what you see is what you get." For introverts, however, the auxiliary function may be even more obvious to others than the dominant one. In a sense, this is because it is often not easy for others to see what introverts "do best." But since the outer world exerts its demands on introverts as well as extraverts, the introvert may be forced to develop his auxiliary function even more than the extravert. For this reason, introverts may appear and communicate more through their auxiliary functions than their dominant ones. As we will see later, this is known as their communication or relational *style*.[17]

THE TERTIARY FUNCTION

The third, or tertiary, function is theoretically even less available than the auxiliary function, since it is usually even less developed. It has the same attitude as the auxiliary and is the opposite function. Therefore, because Ted's auxiliary function is introverted sensation, his tertiary function would be introverted intuition. According to some theorists, since introverts may develop their auxiliary function more than extraverts do, they may have the problem of having the tertiary working in tandem with the least developed function. We will explore this later.

THE INFERIOR FUNCTION

The least developed function is known as the inferior function. It is simply the opposite function pole and opposite attitude of the dominant function. In the case of ESTJ (dominant extraverted thinking), the inferior function is introverted feeling.

As we saw in the diagrams that appear earlier in this chapter, Jung originally conceived of each of the functions as one pole of a bipolar pair. The development of one pole often relates to a *lack of development* of the other pole, almost as if they were mutually exclusive.[18] Because of this oppositional aspect, inherent in the theory of types is the important idea of psychic opposites in need of balancing and differentiation. For example, superior (or dominant) extraverted thinking ideally needs to be balanced or offset with some capacity for introverted feeling.

In this way, typology is a structural approach, a concrete descriptive framework for defining and labeling the various functions of consciousness. It is also a dynamic method of assessing the degree of development and integration of the different and opposing functions within the personality. Understanding some conscious and unconscious features of our particular type enables us to identify our naturally occurring personality—our strengths and weaknesses. Using the dynamic aspect of this model, we can then develop those parts of ourselves in need of strengthening, and balance our more readily available qualities with the less developed ones. The ideal is to develop as much access to all of one's functions as possible.

We can see from this that the inferior function is the last to gain any ascendancy in consciousness (and for many, it never does!). The distance of the inferior function from active consciousness (in that it is embedded in the unconscious) is what makes us call it "inferior." Since it is the complete opposite of the dominant, it also carries the opposite attitude. This means that when a man like Ted primarily uses extraverted thinking, his most undeveloped function is introverted feeling—introverted feeling is both opposite in attitude and function of the dominant. We will return to the inferior function in more detail in chapter 7.

So, for Ted the ESTJ, the dominant function is extraverted thinking, the auxiliary function is introverted sensation, the tertiary function is introverted intuition, and the inferior function is introverted feeling.

For Richard the ISTJ, the dominant function is introverted sensation, the auxiliary function is extraverted thinking, the tertiary function is extraverted feeling, and the inferior function is extraverted intuition.

See table 1 in the appendix for a complete list of all the types and their corresponding attitudes and functions.

SIXTEEN MEN

Much of what I have described so far represents the "hard" theoretical foundation of psychological type. The basic theory of typology offers us a substrate or framework out of which we can begin to appreciate and better understand how some specific nuances of overt behavior are derived.

In order to make these complexities and abstractions of typological theory more concrete and meaningful, I have created a cast of characters, sixteen men representing some behavioral approximations of the sixteen different type profiles in the following chapters. (See table 6 in the appendix for a summary.) These portraits are taken partly from particular individuals, from my personal and clinical experience, and from typological research. Each of these is then followed by a "prototype" representing the more general characteristics we are likely to encounter in the particular type. These characters will be used throughout the book to personify each of the types. I hope this will clarify some of the ideas and bring some of the theory to life.

To begin with, there are eight extraverts and eight introverts (note that there are actually three times as many extraverts as there are introverts in the general population). In our cast of characters, Ted, Jake, Phil, Wally, Paul, Jerry, Sheldon, and Pablo are all extraverts. The introverts are Richard, Harry, Teddy, Cal, Brian, Alexander, Eliot, and Dean.

I hope that by clothing each type in the dress of a character, these descriptions will provide some of the essential flavor of the particular type as well as an idea as to how specific type characteristics might variably manifest in an individual.

I have also provided a commentary on some characteristics of each type, as well as some information on possible interactions with others through each type's communication and relational style.

It is important to remember that neither the characters nor the prototypes are exhaustive or comprehensive definitions of all of the behavioral characteristics of each type. They are more like composite descriptive *possibilities* of both personality and behavior generated out of the individual typological ingredients and their interactions to form an overriding typological character.

A specific intent of providing both a character and a prototype is to avoid the common mistake in the growing literature on typology of oversimplifying individual types by putting them into pigeonholes or, on the other hand, globalizing so much about an individual type that some of its unique flavor is lost in inappropriate and misleading generalizations.

Trying to describe any of the types is complicated because the type profile may not reflect the unique elements of an individual's life experience. Adequate type development results from the optimal use of our individual abilities and life opportunities to maximize our overall psychological growth. In any individual the possible span of development of functions ranges from little development of any of the functions to, more rarely, full development of all of them. So the caveat here is that just because someone is labeled as belonging to a certain type does not mean that that person has achieved a high, or even adequate, development of that function. The key in this regard lies in an individual's ability to consciously differentiate the various functions.

To complicate matters even further, the interactive effect of type and gender roles influence the overt expression of one's type. The freedom to bring any or all of the elements of one's type to full development also depends on the extent to which one adheres to the sex role in which one is raised. For example, feeling type men may not be free to fully express and behave as they would if there were not social constraints against doing so. On the other hand, the behavior and attitudes of thinking type men are likely to be freer, and more fully expressed, since they are more characteristic of conventional masculine sex roles. As we will see later, these social constraints may act against the development of one's full potential, as well as decreasing the likelihood of becoming psychologically androgynous.

Before we meet the sixteen men, I will first describe how psychological types relates to men's communication and relational styles.

CHAPTER 2

Psychological Type and the Ways Men Communicate

One's psychological type is intimately bound to, and expressed through, one's language. Insofar as language is the conventional medium of communication, its role in both effective and disturbed communication is significant. Psychologists and linguists have both studied communication styles and patterns. The field of sociolinguistics often offers helpful guidelines for looking at the social, cultural, and gender-based contributions to communication styles. Yet, we find little in this research explaining the role of psychological type in communication.

As a result, much of the current literature tends to over-attribute communication differences to gender differences. Yet, as we shall see, psychological type is an important dimension of "how" and "what" we communicate. This chapter is a brief explanation of its role in communication.

The overriding typological preference for thinking in men is the most fundamental characteristic underlying social and psychological definitions of conventional "masculinity." This preference has far-reaching consequences for men's behavior, communication styles, and relationships. Likewise, the feeling function in women is the cardinal feature in conventional definitions of "femininity." It is the respective frequencies of these *typological* preferences in men and women that makes it is easy to confuse them with sex differences. Both men and women can be, and are, either thinking or feeling types.

The current linguistic pop fad of "he said/she said" is one example of overgeneralizing from communication styles to sex differences. Deborah Tannen's best seller, *You Just Don't Understand,* is one of several recent books that attribute many of the communication problems between men and women to sex differences. But her descriptions of the way men and women communicate can be understood even more comprehensively as differences in typology, supported by sex-role socialization.

An example from Tannen's book is quoted at length here to illustrate the bias inherent in the linguist's interpretation of sex-related communication styles. She uses Jack Sattel's analysis of a dialogue in Erica Jong's book *Fear of Flying.* Sattel uses the dialogue as an example of the way a man uses silence "as a weapon to exercise power over women."[1]

The first line of dialogue is spoken by Isadora, the second by her husband, Bennett.

"Why do you always have to do this to me? You make me feel so lonely."

"That comes from you."

"What do you mean that comes from me? Tonight I wanted to be happy. It's Christmas Eve. Why do you turn on me? What did I do?"

Silence.

"What did I do?"

He looks at her as if her not knowing were another injury.

"Look, let's just go to sleep now. Let's just forget it."

"Forget what?"

He says nothing.

"Forget the fact that you turned on me? Forget the fact that you're punishing me for nothing? Forget the fact that I'm lonely and cold, that it's Christmas Eve and again you've ruined it for me? Is that what you want me to forget?"

"I won't discuss it."

"Discuss what? *What* won't you discuss?"

"Shut up! I won't have you screaming in the hotel."

"I don't give a fuck what you won't have me do. I'd like to be treated civilly. I'd like you to at least do me the courtesy of telling me why you're in such a funk. And don't look at me that way . . ."

"What way?"

"As if my not being able to read your mind were my greatest sin. I *can't* read your mind. I *don't* know why you're so mad. I *can't* intuit your every wish. If that's what you want in a wife you don't have it in me."

"I certainly don't."

"Then what is it? Please tell me."

"I shouldn't have to."

"Good God! Do you mean to tell me that I'm expected to be a mind reader? Is that the kind of mothering you want?"

"If you had any empathy for me . . ."

"But I *do*. My God, you don't give me a chance."

"You tune out, you don't listen."

"It was something in the movie, wasn't it?"

"What, in the movie?"

"The quiz again. Do you have to quiz me like some kind of criminal? Do you have to *cross-examine* me? . . . It was the funeral scene. . . . The little boy looking at his dead mother. Something got you there. That was when you got depressed."

Silence.

"Well, *wasn't* it?"

Silence.

"Oh come on, Bennett, you're making me *furious*. Please tell me. Please."

(He gives the words singly like little gifts. Like hard little turds.) "What was it about that scene that got me?"

"Don't quiz me. Tell me!" (She puts her arms around him. He pulls away. She falls to the floor holding onto his pajama leg. It looks less like an embrace than like a rescue scene, she sinking, he reluctantly allowing her to cling to his leg for support.)

"Get up!"

(Crying) "Only if you tell me."

(He jerks his leg away.) "I'm going to bed."

Tannen agrees that this scene supports Sattel's belief that Bennett uses his silence as a weapon against his wife. Further, she says that even if one reversed the gender of the characters, "it is hard to imagine a man begging his wife to tell him what he did wrong." However, I think it a misinterpretation to see the dialogue as one in which Isadora is trying to get Bennett to tell her "what she did wrong." That was the relational impact of the dialogue, not its content. The content was about what Bennett was feeling and his difficulty in expressing it. Isadora idiosyncratically interpreted his silence as a punishment. Although it certainly must have felt that way to her, Bennett's inability to express his feeling was his problem, not hers. I have witnessed an exact reversal of couple's dialogues in therapy many times. This conversation could just as easily describe a difference in the communication styles of opposing types, regardless of their sexes.

If we look at it from the perspective of their probable types, their painful dialogue is easier to understand. It appears that Isadora is an extraverted feeling type and Bennett an introverted thinking type, or even an introverted feeling type. (I strongly doubt he was an extravert.) As an extraverted feeler, Isadora naturally wants to know what Bennett is feeling. But since she does not know the nature or significance of his type, she insists that he *express* what he is feeling. With an awareness of typology, she might have approached him differently. She might have understood that discussing his feelings is probably the most difficult thing for him to do. Her insistence only makes matters worse.

On the other hand, with some psychotherapy and some knowledge of typology, Bennett may have been able to understand why he was caught once again in a dilemma all too familiar to him. Typically, both introverted thinking type men and introverted feeling type men are reticent in discussing their feelings. In addition, most of them have been socialized *not* to speak about their emotional vulnerability. These emotionally restrained introverted types are often judgmentally labeled (especially by extraverts) as "passive-aggressive," "withholding," and even "anal." Perhaps that's why Erica Jong referred to Bennett's words as "little turds." Extraverted feeling types are especially likely to feel victimized when they experience introverts as withholding something that, for them, is so easy to give.

One could as easily argue that rather than trying to exercise power over Isadora, Bennett, by remaining silent, was attempting to protect himself from feeling ovewhelmed by his own emotional vulnerability. His need for protection is not any more "right" than her need to force him to express himself. At the only point in the dialogue where he did begin to speak (interestingly, about her lack of empathy), she interrupted him. We could also argue that because of her insensitivity to Bennett's dilemma, Isadora was using verbiage to force Bennett to do what *she* wanted him to. In doing so, she could be seen as controlling, intrusive, and verbally assaultive. With the genders reversed, most women would likely see Bennett as intrusive and belligerent.

Besides suggesting this other point of view of the situation, I would also wonder about Isadora's and Bennett's mutually unconscious motivation in marrying such opposites types. This dialogue between them was obviously not a first; it was likely a recurring problem. It is also one that, in a highly negative way, reinforces and entrenches their opposing differences in communicating.

LANGUAGE AND TYPE

Perhaps what Deborah Tannen calls *genderlect* might more understandably and appropriately be called *typolect.*

Other books on linguistics make the same error of over-ascribing language patterns to actual sex differences rather than to a combination of gender and type. In *Sex Differences in Human Communication,* for example, Barbara Eakins and Gene Eakins describe sex differences in language such as the following:

> Men's speech tends to be more centered around external things and is more apt to involve straight factual communication. It is more literal, direct, and to the point. It employs stronger statements and forms that tend to press compliance, agreement, or belief on the listener.

The same authors describe women's language this way:

Women's speech tends to be more person-centered and concerned with interpersonal matters. It is apt to deal with the speaker's and others' feelings. It is more polite, more indirect, and uses the method of implication. It employs qualifiers and other softening devices to avoid imposing belief, agreement, or obedience on others through overly strong statements, questions or commands.

In the same book the authors further state that men's speech style is

direct, relatively strong in tone, fact bound, and one which thrives on evidence. . . . [A]rgumentation behaviors [are] . . . considered primarily male characteristics, rather than standard behavior for both sexes.

Male dialogue is often weighted by an insistence that statements be based on straight-line reasoning.

And they write that in women's speech

personal opinion, attitudes, and personality are more important for women than fact-bound information. Presumably, they prefer talk that is intimate and personal, dealing with how they think and feel . . . [and they are] less likely to have a hard factual background or to be in contact with the world of knowledge.

And on men and women together, they write:

Women . . . may view men's argumentative style as wearing or too competitive. . . . [T]o some males, women's speech sometimes seems peripheral or off center: "She's totally illogical!" To men, women's dialogues often seem mindless or superficial, mere recitals of feelings. To women, women are sharing a kind of emotional resolution and comfort in their conversation. . . . [E]ach woman comments upon the other's feelings by reflecting them in her responses.

[W]hen they talked to each other, males tended to argue and the females tended to elaborate on each other's utterance. . . . [M]ales would dispute the other person's utterance or ignore it, while the females would acknowledge it or often build on it.

[W]omen used accommodative strategies and men used exploitative ones. . . . [W]omen used obliging, favoring, or adjustive tactics, and the men employed more selfish devices calculated for self-advantage or profit. . . . [W]omen strove for a fair outcome, acceptable to all, whereas men were primarily geared toward winning.[2]

In spite of the authors' extensive research in linguistics, from the foregoing group of quotes it appears as if they have never encountered men who use feeling as a communication style, or women who use thinking as a communication style. In the above quotes one could often replace the phrase "women's speech" with "feeling speech," and "men's speech" with "thinking speech." Much of what is described above as male and female speech is virtually interchangeable with what, in typology, would be called thinking and feeling communication and relational styles.

Sex roles profoundly influence the communication styles of men and women. Typology has been assumed to be part of one's constitution. Whether men and women can be socially liberated enough to express and develop the fullness of their natural type is a matter of conjecture. For example, as we saw with Bennett above, some men who are feeling types may not find it socially appropriate to express themselves in ways that are actually quite natural for them. They might feel more comfortable communicating in their preferred style if there were not rigid social sanctions against men behaving in ways described as "feminine," "soft," or "touchy-feely." Likewise, women who prefer to communicate with a thinking style might also experience social disapproval in doing so. Socially inflexible sex roles discourage the full expression everyone's natural typological preferences.

The four indices in the nucleus of a type, ST, SF, NT, and NF, create special communication qualities, or styles, in the members of each group. *Communication style* describes the way a particular type conveys specific contents of a communication. Each of the indices has four type members. Knowing the nucleus of the group makes the communication styles of its members more predictable.

The STs are more frequently encountered in men; the SFs, in women. Most men's communication styles are composed of S and T. Thinking is men's most typical and frequent communication style. Different combinations of the type nucleus make for varying degrees of similarity.

Men who are ESFJ, ENFJ, ISFJ, or INFJ types are very likely to use the communication style described above as "female." And although to a lesser degree, men who are ESFP, ENFP, ISFP, and INFP are likely to have a style that uses feeling together with a perceiving process. All men with FJ in their type use feeling as their dominant mode of communication, but always to some degree in combination with a perceiving process, either sensation or intuition.

On the other hand, FP men use feeling communication as well, but their primary or secondary preference—sensation or intuition—has a greater influence. For example, the INFP uses feeling in conjunction with his more dominant communication style, intuition, with intuition usually more obvious. His intuition is counterbalanced by feeling. The reason for this is that judging preferences, whether thinking or feeling, always occur in a context of "what" is judged. If it is *possibilities* that are judged by feeling, then the style will be NF. If it is *facts* that are judged by thinking, the style will be ST.

On the other hand, women who are ESTJ, ENTJ, ISTJ, or INTJ types will be quite likely use the more "male"—in other words, thinking—communication style described above. To a lesser degree, women who are ESTP, ENTP, ISTP, and ISTP may also use a more thinking style, but overshadowed by their more dominant intuition or sensation.

TYPE DISTRIBUTION DIFFERENCES IN MEN AND WOMEN

We have seen that contrary to popular opinion, it is more than simply sex differences that account for difficulties in effective communication and relationships. The differences in the frequency of specific types among men as well as in the distribution of types in both men and women have considerable consequences on the overall effectiveness of communication. These differences account for many of the communication difficulties between men and women of different types. Communication problems occur between men and women of dissimilar type, but they also occur in same-sex, different-type interactions.

For example, while the most frequent male type is the extraverted thinking type, ESTJ, the most common type among women is the extraverted feeling type, ESFJ. Almost 50 percent of women have the SF nucleus, and SF women outnumber SF men over two to one. Because there are twice as many SF women as SF men, women are obviously going to encounter and communicate effectively with many more women who are typologically similar to themselves than they will men. We can see from this that for women, opportunities to communicate poorly with ESTJ men are going to be about equal to their opportunities to communicate effectively with other women. The same is, of course, true for men. ST men's opportunities to communicate effectively with other men are equal to their opportunities to communicate poorly with women.

On the other hand, an ISTJ woman will encounter and communicate with very few other women of this type. And INFP and INFJ men will meet and effectively communicate with only a few other men like themselves. From these facts we can see that problems of communication are not as much sex-related as they are type-related. However, because of overall preference patterns in typology, they can easily *appear* to be gender-related. Typological differences make for large variations in both communication and relational styles between men and women.

COMMUNICATION STYLES

To a greater or lesser extent, we all use each of the type functions. However, a particular type preference results in a particular communication style. This communication style is represented by the core, or nucleus, of the type. It is unlikely that there are "pure" communication styles based on only one preference. Rather, thinking or feeling are used alongside either sensation or intuition. We can conclude from the distribution of type among the sexes that many men use communication styles centered around thinking processes, and many women use communication styles centered around feeling. But both styles do exist in both sexes.

In typological terms, a communication style may be expressed primarily through thinking, sensation, intuition, or feeling. Like radio signals, communication can be "sent" in one function and "received" either in the same style or a divergent one. Those communications sent and received in the same style are likely to be effective, those sent and received in divergent styles are likely to be misinterpreted or misunderstood. Because of this, learning to communicate more effectively means being able to shift communication styles. But this learning has to be based on understanding one's own type as well as the type of the listener.

In order for effective communication to occur, both the speaker and the listener must be able to use at least one of the typological functions used by the other. The point is to create a certain degree of shared meaning. The ideal, of course, would be that each of them could use each of the four functions at the appropriate time. The most ineffective communications are those that occur between individuals having highly divergent styles who are also unable to shift to the style of each other, or at least to listen in the style of the speaker.

For example, individuals with ST at the core of their type communicate with either thinking or sensation. They communicate best with other STs because very little shift in style is required of either of them. STs communicating with NTs may require more of a shift than with other STs, particularly when one uses thinking more dominantly and the other uses sensation. STs who do not make a major shift in communicating with SFs will frequently not be heard. STs will generally have the worst time trying to communicate with NFs because there is no common function in the core of either of their types. The same goes for SFs and NTs.

A description of each of the communication styles of the major type groups will be given in the appropriate chapters.

LISTENING AS A METHOD FOR
EFFECTIVE COMMUNICATION

Flavil Yeakley is a psychologist who has studied communication styles as they pertain to psychological type. For each of the sixteen types he has developed "communication style preferences" based on the similarity of functions each of the types used in an extraverted way.

From his preliminary research he has concluded that "effective communication" is "the process of creating an acceptable degree of shared meaning between people."[3] To facilitate that, he developed descriptive styles of listening to be used as guidelines for effective communication.

Yeakley has outlined the specific questions a listener needs to ask about each of the communication styles related to type function. He suggests the following questions in relation to listening to the different styles.

Listening in the sensing style means *interpreting* at a very practical level and asking such questions as:

What is the speaker saying?
How should the words be decoded?
How should the message be perceived?

Listening in the intuitive style means *understanding* at a much deeper level and asking such questions as:

What does the speaker really mean?
What are the assumptions underlying the message?
What are the implications of the message?
What are the possibilities suggested by the message?

Listening in the thinking styles means *analyzing and organizing* while asking such questions as:

What is the structure of the message?
What is the central idea?
What are the main points?
What are the subpoints?
How are the various points related?
Is there adequate evidence to justify each claim?
Is the reasoning logical?
Are the claims true or false?

Listening in the feeling style means *evaluating and appreciating* while asking such questions as:

What values are suggested by the message?
Should these values be accepted or rejected?
How do I feel about the message?
How do I feel about the speaker?[4]

It is clear from these suggested ways of listening that communication styles reflect complex psychological type differences, not simply sex differences.

RELATIONAL STYLES

Communication styles give rise to what I call *relational* styles. While communication styles convey content, a relational style conveys the *impact* of the communication style on the listener. The relational style arises from the nucleus of the type just as it does in the communication style. Problems in communication arise from the overall impact the communication has on the listener, not only out of the content of what is communicated. Like the communication style, the impact of a relational style is often related to differences in the sender's and listener's type cores. Communications between divergent styles are more likely to have a negative impact. Communications between similar styles are more likely to have a positive impact because they are likely to have greater "syntality"—that is, the mental and behavioral features of the group, in other words, the type core, will have greater correspondence to the personality of the individual. Generally, of the possible core types ST, NT, SF, and NF, those communicators with identical cores will have the highest level of rapport. Those varying on only one function, for example, STs, and NTs, or SFs, and NFs, will have the next best level of rapport. And those completely opposite, STs and NFs, or SFs and NTs, will have the least rapport. So theoretically, STs communicating with NFs, and NTs communicating with SFs will have the most difficulty. As we will see later, the other components of type, extraversion and introversion, and judging and perceiving, influence rapport level as well.

We can see how similarity or difference in type styles might affect the quality and degree of persuasion, rapport, and empathy between people. Similarity in communication and relational style creates a sense of "likeness" between people, which leads to an ease in being together. In the example of Isadora and Bennett, here is a low level of "likeness," particularly in the thinking-feeling difference. In fact, they probably perceive each other as alien. Neither feels empathy for the other, so neither feels understood or cared for.

If Isadora and Bennett were being counseled as a couple, we would observe that much of their communication disagreement and dissatisfaction arises from their differences in their relational styles—the impact or effect of how they speak—as well as from what they say. Impacts can be powerful, but subtle. They are difficult to identify because they are not carried by words, but more subtly by emotion, nonverbal language, or innuendo. They are different for each of the major type groups, whose relational styles will be described in the appropriate chapters.

CHAPTER 3

The Thinkers: Ted, Richard, Jake, and Harry

FREQUENCY OF THE THINKERS: 41%

It is intriguing that our first group of men, those with sensation-thinking as the inner core of their type, represent the majority of American men. These four ST types—two thinking types and two sensation types—make up over 40 percent of the male population in the United States. The approximate frequency of individual ST types is ESTJ, 17 percent; ISTJ, 9 percent; ESTP, 9 percent; and ISTP, 6 percent.

Men who have ST as the nucleus of their type also outnumber ST women by almost two to one (see table 4 in the appendix). It is the presence of the thinking preference in this particular type group that creates the disproportionately high number of STs among men. The sensation preference occurs equally among men and women, and those who have NT rather than ST as the nucleus of their type account for only 20 percent of men. However, the ST and NT men taken together account for at least 60 percent of men. Some research sources estimate that the overall frequency of the thinking preference in males may be as high as 65 to 70 percent.[1]

AN OVERVIEW OF THE THINKERS

In this chapter we will meet the ESTJ Ted, a bank officer and the father of Teddy (whom we will meet later); Richard, an ISTJ, who is an accountant who works with Ted; Jake, an ESTP, who is a carpenter working on Ted's kitchen; and Harry, an ISTP, who is a repairman at Ted's bank. (See table 8 in the appendix for a summary of each man's dominant and auxiliary function and communication style.) The description of each of these character types will be followed by a proto-type analysis that will describe the more general characteristics of each type in the ST group. (This will be the format of the next three chapters as well.)

Of the four types I have called the Thinkers, two of them—Ted and Jake—are extraverts. Ted (ESTJ) is called an extraverted thinking type and Jake (ESTP) is called an extraverted sensation type. The other two, Richard and Harry, are introverts. Richard (ISTJ) is called an introverted sensation type, and Harry (ISTP) is called an introverted thinking type. We can see from this that while I call the ST group the Thinkers, there is one extraverted thinker and one introverted thinker, but also an extraverted sensation type and an introverted sensation type. So, the Thinkers group actually consists of two thinking types and two sensation types.

What all of the men in this group "do best" is related to the ST nucleus of their type rather than their designated type name. All of the STs have some measure of heightened thinking and sensation. All of these men appear to focus and rely on objective facts, which they verify through their *senses:* "seeing, hearing, touching, counting, weighing, measuring."[2]

As STS, all of them use sensation over intuition as their way of perceiving, and use thinking over feeling as their way of judging or evaluating what they perceive. As a consequence, they all have some measure of undeveloped feeling and intuition as well. For the two thinking types of this group, Ted and Harry, the feeling function is their least developed ability, and intuition is their tertiary function, second to their least developed function. For the two sensation types, Jake and Richard, intuition is the least developed of their abilities and feeling is their tertiary function.

All of the STS prefer to use thinking processes in combination with sensation. Their preference is to primarily use sensation as a perceptual process and thinking as an evaluative process. This ST preference gives their overall mental process a quality characterized by concreteness, objectivity, and practicality. Whether introverted or extraverted, the "impersonal analysis of concrete facts" is the ST group's forte.

> ST people rely primarily on sensing for purposes of perception and on thinking for purposes of judgment. Their main interests focus on facts, because facts can be collected and verified directly by the senses — by seeing, hearing, touching, counting, weighing, and measuring. The ST types typically approach their decisions regarding facts by impersonal analysis, because what they trust is thinking, with its step-by-step logical process of reasoning from cause to effect, from premise to conclusion.[3]

Each function of consciousness also has a particular orientation to time. Sensation types' orientation to time is largely to the present. For thinking types, that relation to time is a linear one as well — that is, they relate past to present to future.[4]

It is the combination of sensation and thinking that imparts the particular qualities of men who "focus their attention on facts and handle these with impersonal analysis. They tend to be practical and matter-of-fact, and they successfully use their abilities in technical skills dealing with facts, objects, and money."[5]

So, all Thinkers operate by an objective process of sifting and sorting through all of the facts in order to weigh the evidence for the particular decisions they need to make. Theirs is a search for causal explanations, for why something is so. Their decisive natures are literally "ruled" by logic, rationality, and objectivity. Their dominant mental processes tend to be characterized by firmness and attention to the logical and consistent development of thought and precision skills. When this firmness is overdeveloped, it results in rigidity and a tendency toward dogmatism.

ST types tend to be uncomfortable with the emotions of others as well as their own. Often they deny, ward off, or suppress emotional reactions in favor of the more "logical" ones. These particular thinkers and sensation types often have an underdeveloped interpersonal awareness that can result in insensitivity to others' feelings and emotional needs.

COMMUNICATION STYLES OF THE STs

As we will see, the interactions of the various combinations of all the elements of the type profile create the unique flavor of each type. Out of these interactions also arise characteristic communication and behavioral differences. So, what this ST nucleus gives each of the four Thinkers is an interpersonal quality that is best described by their communication and relational style.

The communication style of the STs is characterized by

impersonal, logical reasoning that focuses largely on factual content. The content of the style involves direct messages about the realisitic, concrete aspects of the subject. The language of STs is highly specific and tends to be emotionally barren. Consequently, feeling expressiveness is blunted, controlled, or invisible to the listener. STs also separate or minimize emotional aspects of messages coming from the speaker. They may even note or point out that the emotional "loading" of a speaker's content is irrelevant, or inappropriate to the facts of the communication. This particular communication style is the one most often stereotypically identified as "the way *men* talk"—although, even if less frequently, it is also used by ST women.

Communication style is a way of understanding similarities as well as differences among the different types and type groups. All of the STs favor some combination of thinking and sensation. How they balance the two varies according to the overall type. The two TJs, Ted (ESTJ) and Richard (ISTJ), communicate largely through thinking; and the two TPs, Jake (ESTP) and Harry (ISTP), communicate most often through sensation. Because Ted is an extravert, his communication and relational style is directly through his dominant function, thinking, but this is also combined with sensation. Because of this, Ted tends to communicate in terms of logical, objective processes that have some practical function. Richard, too, uses his thinking in an outer way. He is a "principle seeker." But, rather than organize others in the outer world, as Ted does, he seeks to organize information and ideas more inwardly. Since he is an introverted sensation type, he doesn't ordinarily use sensation as his dominant communication or relational style. Like all introverts, what he uses more often to communicate is the secondary preference—in his case, extraverted thinking. Like Ted, his communication style is also through thinking, but it comes indirectly through his second-best function. So we say that the communication style of both Ted and Richard is thinking, but in combination with sensation.

On the other hand, Jake's ESTP communication style and Harry's ISTP communication style is sensation. Like Ted, the other extravert in the group, Jake (ESTP) communicates directly through his most favored function, which for him is sensation. As an extravert, he also tends to communicate objectively with an eye toward practicality. On the other hand, the other ST introvert, Harry (ISTP), uses his thinking in an inner way. Secondary extraverted sensation is his primary communication style. The quality of Harry's communication style is not only colored by his thinking processes, but in his case more obviously by sensation. An example of this can be seen in Harry's response to his wife's tearful story of breaking a favorite piece of china while cleaning it. Bypassing her hurt feelings, he says, "Well, you should have held onto it tighter (sensation). Besides, that slippery cleaning stuff you use isn't the best cleaner anyway (thinking)."

We can see from the above that together, the dominant and auxiliary functions create a communication style that can be identified even more clearly than simply describing it as a thinking style. Thus, the way the thinking types use their thinking skills in communication is not always the same. For example, Sheldon (ENTJ), an extraverted thinker whom we will encounter later, has NT rather than ST as the nucleus of his type. Even though we call Sheldon an extraverted thinking type, we will see in chapter 3 that his communication style is different from, for instance, Ted's or Jake's.

RELATIONAL STYLES OF STs

STs view relationships in a traditional, conservative way. Realism, and at times pessimism, pervade their attitudes about relationships. They often look for and expect explicit signs of commitment. Their care for others is demonstrated largely through material things—in being able to provide secure, comfortable homes, and possessions, for example. They favor relationships that are stable and predictable. Their expectations of partners are usually clear. If their expectations are not met in what they think are reasonable ways, they become critical of their partners. Their communication style may strike the listener as impersonal, distant, emotionally cool, or overintellectualized, depending, of course, on how similar or different the communication and relational style of the listener is. For example, two people who both have an ST nucleus in their type are generally likely to feel a higher level of rapport and understanding than they will with others having a different type nucleus.

In general, most types with the same nucleus have a better chance for effective communication than those who are not so matched. It is even possible to rank the relative levels of difficulty in communicating based on the nucleus of the respective types. STs will have a little less ease of communication with NTs than with other STs. STs will have even more difficulty with SFs, and the most difficulty with NFs. The ease or difficulty in communicating is more complex when the communication occurs between men and women of differing type nuclei.

TED: AN EXTRAVERTED THINKING TYPE: ESTJ

Ted is a good example of an ESTJ. He is an extravert who prefers judging (specifically thinking over feeling) rather than perceiving, so we call him an extraverted thinking type. This means that extraverted thinking is what he does most of, and what he does best. It imparts a specific quality to his communication style. So we say extraverted thinking is his dominant process. On the other hand, introverted sensation is what he does second best. This secondary function provides him some access to his inner world and helps to balance his primarily extraverted judging approach to the outer world. So, we call his second best function of introverted sensation his auxiliary function.

In many ways the life of an ESTJ child is one of the most structured and orderly. Even as a child, Ted already seemed "too grown up." He learned the meaning of responsibility practically as soon as he learned how to play. Play frequently came only after meeting his obligations. His parents rewarded him for hard work and self-discipline, so achievements quickly came to play a large part in how he learned to value himself. He learned early on that "who" he was and what he accomplished were closely tied together. He was the Eagle Scout with the most merit badges and a frequent winner of science projects at school.

Today, Ted is a successful forty-nine-year-old senior bank officer who has worked for the same bank since graduating from business school. His efficiency, attention to detail, and ability to conceptualize plans and carry them out, as well as his natural leadership abilities, have helped him to rise rapidly in position within the bank.

He has high performance expectations of himself as well as of those he supervises. While he can be congenial and outgoing, he commands respect as a "no-nonsense" manager whose priorities at work are clear to everyone around him. His pet peeves are carelessness and inattention to details. Ted can grow impatient when others haven't fully worked out the details of their ideas before presenting them to him, and he has difficulty fully attending to points of view and feelings unlike his own. He prefers that others agree with his point of view.

Rather dryly, Ted describes his marriage of twenty-five years as "satisfactory and stable." There are few major ups and downs to his family life; he prides himself on being able to provide the financial security and stability that he believes are the foundation of married life. Ted likes to see his home run with the same efficiency, routine, and attention to detail as his business. He belongs to several civic clubs, is a board member of his church, and enjoys a moderate amount of active involvement in family life. He often takes his sons to ball games and participates in their Scout activities. He reinforces a conformist point of view in his sons and is quick to criticize them for their lack of attention to their possessions, the details of their surroundings, and their chores.

His wife sees Ted as emotionally cool since he is not prone to displays of affection or tenderness. While Ted is particularly vulnerable to criticism and emotional rejection, he rarely expresses hurt feelings or vulnerability. Instead, he prefers to try to ignore those feelings and act as if nothing were wrong. He considers emotionality a form of weakness and a potential loss of control.

When he is under stress, Ted generally resorts to tried-and-true methods for getting things done, often ignoring information that could help him in the process. The result is that his approach to a new problem can be rigid. Under sustained emotional pressure he sometimes does lose control, and suffers momentary emotional outbursts because of the ongoing neglect of his feeling side.

Perhaps more than any other type, Ted represents conventional masculinity in the Western world. His attitudes and values are those most frequently viewed by both men and women as the standard of what is typically "masculine."

THE ESTJ PROTOTYPE (17%)

Thinking → Sensation → Intuition → Feeling

The ESTJ type represents the most common type of American man. If there were a gathering of one hundred men representing the general population there would be at least seventeen of this type present. Because it is the most common type, we can see the influence of this personality on our concepts of masculinity.

The extraverted thinkers direct their thinking skills to the outer world rather than to the inner world of personal ideas and ideals. They are probably the most tough-minded of all the types. They are intellectually active, but emotionally passive. At work, this gives them a decided advantage in productivity and efficiency. They are highly role-defined, sensitive to bureaucratic hierarchy, and like to have clear expectations and guidelines for carrying out their jobs. They are authoritative, assertive, decisive, and competitive.

ESTJs are extremely goal- and task-oriented. They direct high levels of aggressive energy to planning, action, and the implementation of goals. They are often efficiency experts whose theme seems to be to get the job done in the most practical, logical, time-efficient manner possible. They enjoy structure, organization, and predictable routines. Recognition and the rewards of accomplishment keep them seeking new tasks to master.

In dealing with others they tend to be straightforward. They have a no-nonsense approach, and so may seem emotionally cool, if not distant. Unfortunately, their approach to relationships is similar to their approach to work: get the job done and do it right, all on the first try. To others, especially those emotionally close to them, they may seem demanding, aggressive, insensitive, and at times, even intolerant.

As fathers and husbands, they are often loyal, dedicated, and committed to their partners and children. They feel a strong responsibility to live up to their parenting role. Caring is expressed by providing appropriate, sufficient, commodious possessions and property for the family's well-being. Since material possessions have a high degree of appeal to them, they are also likely to want to provide the "best" things for their families.

The home is another ground where the ESTJ can implement his need to organize, plan, and carry out goals. But at home this style of working is obviously unproductive and often leads to resentment by partners and children. The ESTJ father often applies the same standards and rules to his children as he does to himself. He expects his children to demonstrate effort, competency, follow-through, and decisiveness. He dislikes vagaries, inefficiency, and things half-done. For these reasons he can be a persistent taskmaster even at home.

However well intending these fathers are, their children may experience them as exacting, controlling, and demanding. ESTJ fathers often have little idea of what is really "good enough" for themselves. As a result, they often fail to convey what is good enough to their children, and especially to their sons. So while the ESTJ father emphasizes the need for success, he may fail to communicate to his sons what the specific and reasonable goals of success actually are, especially those beyond the material and monetary. Sons of ESTJ fathers usually learn that they are expected to succeed, but they often don't know when or where to stop.

ESTJs have rarely learned from their *own* fathers how much is "good enough," and this lack of limits seems to be passed through generations of fathers and sons. Without realistic limits, they may rarely achieve the goals they set for themselves to their full satisfaction. They can become very frustrated when they still don't feel fulfilled, even though to all appearances they have succeeded in achieving their goals. The downside of the ESTJ is related to the inferior (undeveloped) function of the type, which is inferior feeling. When ESTJS' compulsive approach to both work and home is untempered, they become increasingly burdened with unfair demands. Life may become an endless series of outer tasks to be mastered, with little pleasure reaped from fulfilling individual inner goals. Their high levels of expectation are tied directly to their feelings of self-worth and self-esteem. They are often experienced by others as uncompromising, unappreciative taskmasters who rarely value the efforts made to please them. Yet the demands they make on themselves can be just as uncompromising.

Because the mind of an ESTJ is so busy, he finds it hard to relax and take time for himself, to let down and let go. When he does not take the time to balance his compulsive expectations with leisure and relaxation, he may develop stress-induced symptoms and physical problems. Yet even when an ESTJ begins to break down, it is not easy for him to admit to his vulnerabilities and limits. Consequently, he may go too long before seeking help from others. Needing help in solving his own problems may feel to him like a personal failing.

Often only at the end of their lives, when there is finally time for them to become introspective, do ESTJS turn to their emotional and spiritual needs. Their late-life self-assessment may lead them to realize that they had many more interpersonal options and possibilities than they were able to see during their "busy" years. At retirement, in spite of their outer world accomplishments, they often haven't found fulfillment in their most important relationships. When this happens, they are among the most disillusioned of all the types.

ESTJ men traditionally have the most conventionally masculine orientation to themselves as well as to the outer world. Of all the types of men, it is the extraverted thinkers with sensation who need most to define realistic expectations and limits for themselves. This is so because they are most likely to define success and happiness as being derived from who they are, what they accumulate, and what they do outwardly. They are unlikely to value themselves for their emotional or spiritual qualities.

FREQUENT OCCUPATIONS OF ESTJs

Bank officer	Sales manager
Financial manager	Trade and technical teacher
Auditor	School administrator
Manager	Factory and site supervisor
Supervisor	Surgeon
Judge	Pathologist
Lawyer	Public service aide
Military serviceman	Government worker
Police officer	Insurance agent
Detective	Underwriter
Sales representative	

RICHARD: AN INTROVERTED SENSATION TYPE: ISTJ

Richard is an ISTJ—one of the types whose dominant function, introverted sensation, is Ted's auxiliary function. (Also, as we saw above, Ted's primary function—extraverted thinking—is Richard's auxiliary.) He uses judging with sensation and thinking.

As a child, Richard was an "ideal" student who frequently got As in most of his classes. He was neat, organized, and independent, and he didn't need to be nagged to do homework. While he liked to have the necessary directions for what was expected of him, he disliked needlessly long or superfluous explanations. He seemed to genuinely enjoy meeting the challenges and expectations of being a student. He particularly enjoyed math and science. At home he could often be found in his room, studying, working on his stamp collection, or quietly listening to the radio. His room conveyed some of the qualities of his personality—neat, organized, even a bit austere. He seemed eager to please his parents, seeking out projects he thought would meet their approval.

As a teenager Richard continued in much the same style he developed as a young boy. In sports he was more often an observer than a participant. Socially he felt awkward, especially with girls. He was shy and uncomfortable with the prospect of asking girls out, though he very much wanted to do that. Eventually he did meet a rather bright and extraverted girl who seemed to know how to draw him out. This relationship lasted all through high school and into his first year of college.

Richard's early intellectual life seems almost precocious compared to his emotional development. As a child and a teenager he seldom gave vent to strong feeling, and often one wouldn't know without asking if he was emotionally moved. Whether this was due to the fact that his father rarely showed his own emotional responses or whether Richard just seemed to have a less emotional disposition than others is unclear.

Today, Richard works with Ted at the bank, in the accounting department. Although he is an introvert, Richard probably gets along with Ted better than any other type. Of all the types, these two seem to be closest in values, purposes, and point of view. In American society they are likely to be the most conservative and "macho" appearing of the all male types.

There is a natural compatibility between many of the types where the dominant function of the extravert is the introvert's secondary function. This is largely because with this combination the communication style of the two types is the same. Ted respects and gets along well with Richard because both of their most available functions are the same even though they use them somewhat differently. That is, they both use introverted sensation and extraverted thinking. Ted communicates using thinking since he is an extraverted thinking type; and because he is an introvert, Richard also uses thinking as his way of communicating outwardly.

Like Ted, Richard is very well organized and likes to plan ahead. He is responsible, results-oriented, and not much interested in abstract thinking issues. Ted knows he can depend on Richard to be there when it counts most. When Richard reviews the accounting routines, he rarely misses the details that Ted has a tendency to overlook. Ted appreciates Richard's thoroughness when these details are brought to his attention. Both have a high regard for accuracy. At the bank, Richard has a proven record of dependability, responsibility, and dedication. He knows the rules and regulations of the organization and abides by them, often to the letter. He is often ruled by conventional expectations of how his job should be carried out; he also expects others to respect them and follow suit.

Richard's dominant introversion is one of the few traits that he does not share with Ted. Because of his rather quiet, reserved demeanor he remains somewhat tolerant of Ted's authority, as long as he is left to work largely by himself. Like other ISTJs, his quiet exterior often belies an inner intensity.

Even though he prefers to remain an introvert, Richard can be outgoing when the situation demands it. He has an abundance of social grace and verbal skill that helps him interact with others in personally and professionally appropriate ways. While he has a well-adapted outer persona, like Ted he is basically emotionally reserved and usually not spontaneous with others. Because of this Richard is actually not easy to know well until there is time to establish familiarity and develop friendship.

THE ISTJ PROTOTYPE (9%)

Sensation → Thinking → Feeling → Intuition

Men with introverted sensation and extraverted thinking are most dedicated to what they do as long as what they are doing makes logical sense to them. Both their logic and attention to detail make them among the most painstaking, dedicated, and organized of men. They honor their commitments. Their sense of achievement comes through completing the goals they set for themselves in the best possible way they can. They can be burdened by perfectionistic tendencies. In this regard they have a similar problem to the ESTJs—they often don't know the meaning of "good enough."

Because of their introversion, ISTJs have the same relational style as ESTJs. That is, they most often use extraverted thinking—which is their auxiliary function—to relate and to communicate. This makes them particularly compatible with ESTJs. Even though they are introverts, they often have an unusual social grace. They are at ease verbally and can even be outgoing because they often have a well-developed persona.

Like the ESTJs, behind their persona they can be macho, austere, and not as spontaneous as they first appear to be.

Intellectually, they are impatient with theory and don't place much stock in abstractions. Instead, they prefer tangible, pragmatic applications of concrete facts to a specific task or problem. They are collectors of information and objective data, which they translate according to the task at hand. They have an inner focus oriented to the here and now.

In their work they are organized, systematic, analytic, and scheduled. They prefer to work alone. Although they are sensible, they can be driven and impatient. They are action-oriented, like routines, and like a place for everything.

The ISTJ is a loyal, dutiful, and responsible father who is strongly committed to ensuring the security and safety of his family. Yet even with family members he tends to be emotionally reserved. His caring is often expressed through carrying out his responsibilities to the family in general, and to its individual members, in particular. He can do this without demonstrating a great deal of affection or warmth.

The ISTJ likes his home neat, efficient, organized, and run according to predictable routines. Because of this he can be demanding at home, governing his family's behavior with a set of "shoulds" similar to those he confers on himself. He often establishes rules and regulations and holds his children accountable for following them to the letter of the law. Because he is so action-oriented, he strongly dislikes apathy, idleness, disorganization, and sloppiness.

When an ISTJ father happens to have children who are less persevering and demanding of themselves than he is, problems may result. Children who are more easygoing and appear laid back may be seen by an ISTJ father as lazy, undisciplined, or unmotivated. An ISTJ father who drives himself very hard, often with unrealistic expectations, may become resentful of a child, particularly a boy, who by his father's standards, just doesn't seem to care.

So, on the downside, the ISTJ father's difficulty in allowing himself time for relaxation and leisure may result in compensatory attitudes in his children that take them to the other extreme. His children may not only resist his demands as unrealistic, but become even more complacent. These children commonly perceive their fathers as rigid, controlling, demanding, and generally "uptight." The result can be that neither father nor child feels appreciated, valued, or understood by the other. This is further complicated by the fact that the ISTJ father is emotionally unprepared to openly express affection to his children. Because he uses a relational style based on thinking, he can express his objective, factual expectations, but is handicapped when it comes to expressing feelings of warmth and tenderness to his children.

FREQUENT OCCUPATIONS OF ISTJs

Accountant	Electrician
Auditor	First line supervisor
Administrator	Mathematics teacher
Manager	Trade and technical teacher
Dentist	Mechanical engineer
Police officer	Steel worker
Police supervisor	Technician
Detective	Cleaning services worker

JAKE: AN EXTRAVERTED SENSATION TYPE: ESTP

Jake, an ESTP, has the same type attitude (extraversion) and the same functions (sensation and thinking) as Ted, the ESTJ, but his lifestyle preference is the more easygoing perceiving rather than judging. His preference for the perceiving way of dealing with the outer world means that he favors sensation over thinking. Because he is an extravert, his dominant function is extraverted sensation. Jake's auxiliary function is introverted thinking.

As a child, Jake was rather restless and had a difficult time in school. He was the child who said, "What's the sense in learning this? I'll never use it." He often needed to be shown the importance of school subjects in very practical, concrete ways. Because of this he was often labeled as having low frustration tolerance, being distractible, and "hyperkinetic." At one point, he was even medicated with Ritalin, a drug for hyperactive children, although it was clear later that he didn't have a learning disability and that he wasn't truly hyperactive. The school environment had low tolerance for high levels of activity, resulting in a negative label for Jake. Situations like these may be why types like Jake have such a difficult time succeeding in school.

Perhaps for these reasons, Jake generally seemed much more interested in being with his friends at recess and after school than being in the classroom. At times he required a tutor, especially for subjects that were more theoretical than practical. He also needed a lot of help in organizing his work, keeping track of details, and remembering assignments. He seemed to do best with manipulation of materials, rather than concepts. And he was at his very best when a class project required making something to demonstrate an underlying principle. In high school he excelled in technical and mechanical shop courses. While Jake started college, he soon dropped out, impatient with the impracticality of what was taught.

Today, Jake is a carpenter who is remodeling Ted's kitchen. Like Ted (ESTJ), he prefers to make decisions based on thinking rather than feeling. However, unlike Ted, he is more easygoing about his decisions. In general, Jake is more spontaneous and action-oriented than Ted. In addition, his perceiving quality makes it easier for him to relax and have more fun. When he's not working he enjoys activities embellished with excitement, adventure, and even chance. At times these attributes make Jake seem far removed from Ted with his penchant for security and stability. Sometimes Ted thinks Jake is overly spontaneous and doesn't think things through enough. At the same time, Ted appreciates and relies on Jake's seemingly uncanny ability to know what will work and what will not in the design of the new kitchen. Jake's sharp observation of details allows him to make spontaneous planning decisions without wasting a lot of time on unimportant, irrelevant, or immaterial information. Being one of the more resourceful of types, Jake also seems to always know where to get just the right tile, cabinet knobs, tools, and gadgets.

Ted sometimes considers Jake to be rather "flaky," if not outright hedonistic. From Ted's point of view, Jake seems impulsive and, compared to himself, much less organized. Being the more gregarious of the two, Jake also likes to "chat" with Ted or whoever happens to be in the kitchen while he works. Jake is particularly fond of Ted's son because they both seem to like to talk about how things are done. Although Teddy is shy, he appreciates Jake's boisterous, friendly personality and his willingness to explain how things work. This sometimes irritates Ted, who thinks that Jake talks so much that the job may never get done. Yet at the end of the day, the project is somehow finished even though Jake seems to have spent more time talking than working. To Ted, Jake also tends to lack diplomacy. He challenges Ted's ideas and is even bluntly critical of them at times. Apart from these differences they otherwise have a good deal in common.

Ted and Jake are both extraverts. What sets them apart is how they respond to the outer world and the way their auxiliary functions differ. Jake's dominant function is extraverted sensation; Ted's is extraverted thinking. On the other hand, Jake's auxiliary function is introverted thinking, while Ted's is introverted sensation. To some extent the auxiliary function balances each of their extraverted approaches to the world by providing some access to inner life and to the world of ideas.

For example, Ted's attraction to tools and gadgets and to doing things around the house derives partly from his introverted sensation. Jake appreciates this about Ted. Besides planning the remodel of Ted's kitchen, they have also discussed other do-it-yourself home projects. As for Jake, he is actually more precise and more oriented to the underlying principles of his work (introverted thinking) than his extraverted sensation would make him appear to be. Jake surprised Ted, for example, with the methodical and precise way he planned and designed the kitchen.

Jake and Ted also have something in common with other men whose dominant function corresponds to their auxiliary function. For example, Ted has some inner characteristics in common with Richard, his accountant, as well as with Brian, his physician. Both Richard and Brian's dominant function is introverted sensation. On the other hand, Jake has characteristics in common with both Harry, a repairman, and Ted's brother Cal, a math professor. Both Harry and Cal's dominant function is introverted thinking.

Although Ted and Jake have almost the same components in their types, in some important ways they are not as similar as they first appear to be. In fact, they are more different from each other than they are from other types whose dominant function parallels their auxiliary function. In addition, what

Ted, Richard, and Brian all have in common is the J (judging) quality: they are all more organized and decisive, and they like things planned ahead of time. Jake, Harry, and Cal all have the P (perceiving) quality in common: they are more spontaneous, less decisive, and usually less organized. These JP characteristics, of course, are also true for introverts.

THE ESTP PROTOTYPE (9%)

Sensation → Thinking → Feeling → Intuition

ESTPs are realistic, practical, and oriented to action. They are consummate pragmatists. They rely on their skills of observation and sensate information gathering to provide an objective, dependable view of the world. They have strong mechanical skills and quickly understand how things work. They are excellent troubleshooters; their approach to solving problems is adaptable, flexible, and resourceful.

Like the ESTJs, ESTPs make their decisions based on thinking. However, because their thinking is introverted, they relate to the world through their dominant function, extraverted sensation. As a result, unrelated theoretical ideas don't mean much to them. Although they can understand underlying principles, they prefer to focus on the practical tasks at hand rather than get involved in figuring things out or explaining them to others. To learn new things they tend to rely on memory rather than on understanding theory. Their lack of tolerance for the theoretical is one of the reasons that formal education is so unappealing to them and why they often don't do well academically.

With others, ESTPs are friendly, outgoing, keenly observant, excitable, and even challenging. They can also be forthright, and sometimes even blunt. ESTPs tend to be lively, spontaneous, and fun-loving. They live much more in the moment than their ESTJ cousins, and are much more easygoing as well. Unlike ESTJs, ESTPs don't seem to have trouble finding time to relax or enjoy themselves. In fact, they seem to finish their work in order to play, which to them involves adventure and some risk taking.

Family life for ESTPs can be a great source of pleasure when the activities are plentiful, stimulating, and involve the whole family. As fathers, they often like active, direct involvement in their children's activities. They make good coaches and Boy Scout leaders. As partners, they are exciting mates, always on the lookout for something new to try. They run the risk of wearing out their more introverted partners with their quest for the next, even more exciting things to do. As extraverted sensation types, they have a particular need to find the sensual, pleasurable, and earthy in their relationships. At times, their partners may find them abrupt, "too physical," and insensitive.

While ESTPs appreciate novelty and spontaneity, they have a penchant for the familiar and predictable. At the same time, they are not particularly good planners and have a tendency to be disorganized. But however disorganized they become, they will always do what needs to be done.

A major downside of ESTPs is that they strongly dislike routines, predictability, and virtually anything unchanging. Their impulsivity and tendency to live too much in the outer, concrete world deters them from introspection, reflectiveness, and long-range planning. Their dislike and disregard of rules, regulations, and procedures can earn them the reputation of being uncooperative and even rebellious. ESTPs need to be able to develop the ability to focus their attention on the ordinary tasks before them. They are often tempted to resist the demands of the moment and go in search of something more stimulating or personally interesting to them.

FREQUENT OCCUPATIONS OF ESTPs

Carpenter	Retail salesperson
Craftworker	Marketer
Farmer	Service worker
Laborer	Transportation operative
Police officer	Auditor
Detective	Manager
Sales representative	Administrator

HARRY: AN INTROVERTED THINKING TYPE: ISTP

Harry, the bank's repairman and building engineer, is an ISTP. His dominant function is introverted thinking and his auxiliary function is extraverted sensation. As a child, Harry had to know the logical reasons for why things were the way they were—for himself. He was intrigued by gadgets, tools, and any kind of mechanical device. He could spend long periods of time taking apart and putting together things that were broken. He also took great pleasure in touching, feeling, and understanding just "how things worked." He was compliant as long as he understood the reasons for the rules. His childhood need to understand the ways things worked carried over into adult life in his interest in mechanics and repair work of different kinds.

Harry takes great pride in his mechanical abilities. Much of his self-esteem comes from being able to work with his hands. He is an independent thinker who likes to understand the principles by which things operate. He tends to be a loner. He has little regard for the bank hierarchy, thinking of himself as separate from the bank's organization, and at times he is almost insubordinate. Others often think of him as being aloof. At work he directs his attention toward getting the job done quickly, not toward interacting with others. His personal philosophy and behavior well exemplify the dictum "live and let live."

One particularly hot summer afternoon the air-conditioning system at the bank went out. Ted, in his typical managerial style, called on Harry to get it running as quickly as possible. He also wanted to know in detail (his extraverted thinking) why the system had failed in the first place, hadn't it failed last summer, and couldn't it have been prevented from breaking down again? Ted's authoritative questioning annoyed Harry because he saw the situation as simply requiring the replacement of a damaged part. (This illustrates his extraverted sensation.)

Though Harry thoroughly understood why the system had broken down, he didn't feel he should be bothered to explain this to Ted. While he takes pride in his ability to understand what went wrong with the system, he doesn't feel compelled to share the information. Because his thinking is introverted, he takes the attitude that if *he* knows what the problem is, that's all that matters. Ted was irked because he assumed Harry didn't even know why the system broke down, and was just hedging. The situation was further complicated because Harry felt that Ted's wanting to know the reasons was just another form of "pulling rank," which he resented. As with other introverted thinkers, Harry's least developed extraverted feeling often makes him prone to moodiness, irritability, and withdrawal from others.

Harry's modus operandi is logical and practical: understand the underlying principle, find out how to apply it, and get the job done, all in the shortest period of time. Since he is not given to abstract thinking, he puts little stock in theorizing about what he's doing. Once he understands (primarily for himself) how to get something fixed, he proceeds as if to find the shortest distance between two points. Others may find him emotionally cool and frustrating to work with since he often doesn't bother to explain what he's doing; he just does it. Unlike an extraverted thinker, he does not display his mental machinery to others. Expediency, not information for its own sake, is his top priority.

Harry's greatest interest is actually outside of his job: he builds and races cars. He spends most of his spare time in this pursuit with his friends, who are all equally interested in using their intelligence and superlative mechanical skills to push their racing cars to their uppermost limit of performance. It is in situations like these that Harry becomes the most animated, friendly, and enthusiastic.

We can see from the example of the interaction between Harry and Ted how easily misunderstandings can occur even when both of the men are thinking types. What stands out about Harry in this encounter is not his superior introverted thinking, but his extraverted sensation. The result is a clash of communication styles. This is an example of what can happen when the dominant functions of two people fail to communicate appropriately—their common undeveloped function creates the potential for trouble.

THE ISTP PROTOTYPE (6%)

Thinking → Sensation → Intuition → Feeling

The ISTP at is first hard to figure. From the outside he appears almost inert, passive, and not very spontaneous. To appreciate the type, one has to see him in action. However, *when* he will spring to action is not always predictable, because he tends to be spontaneous only when there is something to be done. Like the ESTP, he can sometimes even be impulsive. His activities are never aimless, but always task-

and solution-oriented. He measures the energy required for the task carefully and precisely.

Interpersonally, the ISTP is passive, cautious, reserved, and taciturn. His economy in action is matched by his economy in speech. Although he often doesn't say more than is necessary to get the facts across, what he says is usually accurate. As a result, he may appear to be withholding, or even passive-aggressive. He enjoys personal freedom and can become detached and self-absorbed when involved in projects that stimulate his interest. But when there is a problem to be solved or something to be fixed, he is among the most quick responding and outer-directed of the types.

The ISTP is curious, expedient, and practical. Intellectual and theoretical abstractions don't interest him much, so he is not often a high academic achiever. He does like facts, however, especially those that he can integrate and use toward some purpose. However, he tends to dislike routines, deadlines, and procedures, preferring instead to leave things unstructured.

As well as being skilled in mechanics, ISTPs can be very proficient in organizing large amounts of data into understandable entities. They are analytical, observant, and look for causes and effects. They most like concrete applications for the information they gather or classify. Even though they sometimes have a tendency to be disorganized, they can be systematic when information needs to be organized for a purpose. Since they have secondary extraverted sensation, they are highly tactile and make excellent observers. Because of this they learn best from practical, hands-on experience.

As a partner, the ISTP is often emotionally closed and doesn't communicate directly how much he cares. His affection is more likely to be expressed by what he does, than what he says. He does favors, fixes things, buys presents, and always expects that his partner will understand these gestures as expressions of his love. When his gestures aren't acknowledged in the spirit in which they were made, he can become moody because he feels unappreciated and misunderstood. He likes a participatory partner, one who enjoys the same activities and interests as he does.

The ISTP is an active, trusting, and generous father. He likes interactions with his children to be activity-oriented and goal-directed. He expresses his care in practical helpfulness and problem solving, rather than displays of affection or spontaneous attention. Because of this his children often experience him as emotionally cool, even aloof. But his warmth becomes apparent when he can participate in and organize adventurous outings, especially ones that excite his own interests. Outings ignite the ISTP's spontaneity, as well as providing an opportunity to express his fathering and love.

The ISTP's own need for independence and practical realism not only makes him highly individualistic, but reinforces these qualities in his children. He seems to deplore dependency and impracticality. Because of this, he tends to be much easier on his ST sons than on his daughters. Daughters wanting to live up to an ISTP father's expectations will probably have to be ST types themselves, or at least able to be part-time tomboys. Sons of ISTPs who are NF types will find these fathers difficult, and often ultimately have little respect for them if their fathers force them into overly practical situations and pursuits.

On the downside, because ISTPs are either so cautious or indifferent interpersonally, they need to learn better communication skills and ways to achieve greater openness in relationships. They have a tendency to procrastinate, often leaving important decisions for the last minute. They may also become so self-absorbed in their projects that they leave little time for more enjoyable activities.

FREQUENT OCCUPATIONS OF ISTPs

Repairman	Farmer
Carpenter	Mechanic
Construction worker	Military serviceman
Dental hygienist	Probation officer
Electrical engineer	Steelworker
Electrical technician	Transportation operator

SUMMARY OF THE ST GROUP

With these descriptions of the ST types we have accounted for the thinking component when it exists in combination with sensation, as either the dominant or auxiliary function in men's type. We have seen that the STs are particulary well suited to deal with the *impersonal* realm of analyzing problems of procedure, mechanics, methodology, and organization. Their orientation to the world is largely practical, factual, and logical. The presence of the thinking function in its interaction with sensation imparts a stereotyped masculine partiality to this type group. Men with ST at the core of their type outnumber men with NF at the core of their type by at least three to one. Largely by dint of their numbers, as well as by their social and economic dominance, ST men determine conventional ideas of what is the appropriately masculine way to communicate in our society. Because of this, their communication and relational styles are generally accepted as the most socially appropriate ways for *both* men and women to communicate. As we have seen, this particular combination is preferred by over 40 percent of men. Only half as many women belong to the ST group. Among all of the individual types, there are even more dramatic differences between men and women. For example, while Richard's type, the ISTJ, is the second-most common type among men, ISTJ occurs comparatively rarely in women; only one in twenty-three women have that typological configuration. On the other hand, as we will see later, the group most unlike the sensation-thinkers, the intuitive-feeling group, consists of only 14 percent of men. But over 20 percent of women are NFs. The greatest overall typological difference between men and women is that as many as 65 to 70 percent of men prefer thinking and as high as 68 percent of women prefer feeling.

We can break down the male ST group even more closely by looking at their lifestyle preference, J or P. The J or P factor makes for some wide-ranging differences between them.

STJs, like Ted and Richard, account for 25 percent of men and differ significantly from their STP counterparts, Jake and Harry. Men with extraverted thinking and introverted sensation are most removed from the feeling function. Their fellowship revolves more around civic, political, or social functions that are stringently circumscribed by either rules or rituals. Dealings between them are most often restricted to factual, practical matters and don't involve much emotional camaraderie. Because of this, there often isn't much direct and easy emotional interchange with other men or with women. In fact, their deepest feelings are so often removed from their outer expressions and behavior that one might suspect them of being emotionally shallow. Emotional responses of STJ fathers for their sons are particularly blunted, and they are not likely to express their appreciation, admiration, and love for their sons easily. Sons of STJs are often confused when they see their fathers being more comfortable with outer things—a football game or a promotion at work—than about the son's feelings.

Because they are so far removed from their feeling function, these men are not likely to be aware of the playful, regressive parts of themselves. Their own "inner child" is often dampened early in life, as they begin to act responsibly and conscientiously. In fact, fulfilling personal responsibility is a signal characteristic of the type.

STJs loom large among businessmen, managers, and corporate executives who value professional accomplishments above most anything else they do. They may even comprise the majority of "workaholics" and type A personalities. All these men need some regressive qualities in order not to take themselves or their work so seriously.

STPs are quite different from STJs because of their perceiving orientation. For example, while Ted and Richard, as STJs, embody responsibility and structure, Jake and Harry, as STPs, are often equally known for their disorganization and lack of discipline or follow-through. Each of them has a lower tolerance for rules and regulations and are more likely to feel cramped by standard operating procedures. But a major difference between Jake and Harry is obvious in their relationships with others. As an introvert, Harry tends to be more of a loner and appears to be more insensitive to others. Jake is more excitable, usually seeks others out, and is more gregarious and challenging with them. He is more forthright and, at times, can even be blunt. Harry will often remain emotionally quiet until pushed too far, then to everyone's surprise, has a sudden and unexpected burst of anger or resentment.

STPs may not take their work as seriously as STJs. They are more likely to be invested in material possessions, especially those involved in their risky, leisurely pursuits like speed boating, river rafting, and racing cars. Compared to STJs, STPs generally like their work situations and home life to be more reasonable, adaptable, and flexible. But they can be also be impulsive and more interested in finding the unique solution to a problem rather than going by tried-and-true methods.

STP fathers are not likely to be any more emotionally expressive with their sons than the STJs are, but they may include their sons more directly in their "manly" leisure pursuits. Although they are often very observant, these skills don't always carry over to their son's feelings. STP fathers see these shared activities as a primary way to develop their relationships with their sons. They see these activities as "good" for their sons. And even when they aren't, it's difficult for the sons to say so because, after all, they are getting to spend time with their dads, and that's what's most important. Only when a son has grown up will he sometimes admit to not really enjoying his father's activities.

When a son is a very different type than his father, he might agree to activities he doesn't enjoy, but later feel resentful because he didn't feel he had a choice, or didn't want to hurt his father's feelings. A case in point is made by a feeling type patient of mine whose father was an avid hunter. He recalled going hunting with his father and being deeply traumatized by having to shoot a deer on his first hunting trip. He was never able to tell his father that afterward he cried for the deer. Another man I know played football in high school only because his father was a coach and wanted him to. As a feeling type, he resented the fact that football required him to be violent and aggressive.

Next, we will look at the second group of men, the NTs. These "Idea Men," the intuitive thinking types, are those in whom thinking is again either their dominant or auxiliary function. But in NTs, thinking exists in combination with intuition rather than sensation. As we will see, this creates some interesting variations in behavior, attitudes, and interests of these men in contrast to the STs.

CHAPTER 4

The Idea Men: Sheldon, Alexander, Cal, and Paul

FREQUENCY OF THE IDEA MEN: 20%

If we were to return to our gathering of a hundred men, we would find twenty who have intuition and thinking (NT) at the core of their type. These Idea Men are characterized by heightened thinking combined with heightened intuition. Their most typically undeveloped functions are feeling and sensation.

There are half the number of NT (20.2 percent) men as there are ST men. When this NT group is combined with the ST group we can account for over 60 percent of all the types of men. Like the ST group, the overrepresentation of men of this type core reflects male preference for the thinking function. This predominance of the thinking preference in both of these groups also gives them their conventionally "masculine" slant.

The "shadow" group of the NTs are the SFs. Even though most men have thinking in their type more than feeling, because sensation in men is so much more dominant than intuition, there are more SF men than there are NTS. The SF males comprise about 26 percent of men. On the other hand, almost half of women types are SF. Only 9 percent of women share the NT core.

NF men, in whom the feeling function replaces the thinking function and intuition replaces sensation, are the true minority of men—they make up only 13 percent of all men. On the other hand, there are almost *twice* as many NFS among women.

AN OVERVIEW OF THE IDEA MEN

In this chapter, we will meet Sheldon, the school administrator of Teddy's school, an ENTJ; Alexander, a neuropsychologist, an INTJ; Cal, a professor and Ted's brother, an INTP; and Paul, Cal's son, an ENTP. See table 9 in the appendix for a summary of each man's dominant and auxiliary functions. As in the previous chapter, the description of each of these character types will be followed by a prototype that will describe the more general characteristics of each type in the NT group.

Of the four types I have called the Idea Men, two of them, Sheldon and Paul, are extraverts. Sheldon is an extraverted thinking type, and Paul is an extraverted intuitive type. The other two, Alexander and Cal, are introverts. Alexander is an introverted intuitive type, and Cal is an introverted thinking type. We can see from this that while I call the NT group the Idea Men, there is not only an extraverted thinker and an introverted thinker, but also an extraverted intuitive and an introverted intuitive. So the NT group consists of two thinking types and two intuitive types.

What all of the men in this group "do best" is related to the NT nucleus of their type, rather than their designated type name. All of the NTs have some measure of heightened thinking and intuition, and as a consequence of that, some measure of undeveloped feeling and sensation as well. All of the NTs prefer to use thinking processes in combination with intuition. Their preference is to primarily use intuition as a perceptual process and thinking as an evaluative process.

Intuitive types' orientation to time is largely to the future. But as we saw with the STs, thinking types' relation to time is a linear one; that is, they tend to relate past to present to future.[1] Here is a summary of the overall mental processes of the NT group:

> NT people prefer intuition for purposes of perception, but they prefer the objectivity of thinking for purposes of judgment. They too focus on possibilities, theoretical relationships, and abstract patterns, but they judge these with impersonal analysis. Often the possibility they pursue is a technical, scientific, theoretical, or executive one, with the human element subordinated.[2]

I have chosen to call the NTs Idea Men because they are the tireless innovators, constantly seeking new challenges or problems to solve. They thrive on novel ideas; new possibilities are the fuel of their inspirations. The concrete, mundane, and excessively practical routines in life seem like a curse to them.

The extraverts among the Idea Men, Paul and Sheldon, rely on a steady flow of outer projects to keep them busy or interested. They are always on the go, looking for new territory to explore and new solutions to both old and new problems. Their enthusiasm is often a source of inspiration for others. The downside of their types is that, more often than not, they may fail to implement their own ideas, but rather require an army of helpers to carry them out.

The introverted Idea Men, Alexander and Cal, are also

highly innovative but in a more contained or circumscribed way. They have an uncanny and often single-minded capacity to focus on specific projects that spark their particular interests. Once they find these areas of interest, they work with determination to actualize them. They are more excited by their own ideas than by the ideas of others. They tend to be highly individualistic and unless they are careful can become overly caught up in and isolated in their own innovative pursuits, and ignore the interests of others.

COMMUNICATION STYLES OF THE NTs

NTs prefer brief, concise, and well-articulated communications, so much so, they may become pedantic. Like the STs, they prefer objectivity and don't want communication "clouded" by emotional or feeling issues. They don't mind alternative ways of conceptualizing a problem, in fact they avoid tried-and-true methods. They like to argue the many sides of a problem, often resorting to the "devil's advocate" position, if only for the sake of discussion. They are capable of seeing opposing points of view, but more often prefer their own. While they show objectivity, they are always ready to criticize the ideas of others. They are often highly persuasive, if not convincing, in their manner and style of speech. Much of the content of their communication centers around ideas, formulas, tasks, and impersonal events. The more novel the better.

As in the ST group, the two TJs of this group, an extravert, Sheldon (ENTJ), and an introvert, Alexander (INTJ), communicate largely through thinking. Along with the two TJs from the ST group, Ted and Richard, these are the four types who use thinking as a communication style. These four TJs make up a separate grouping of men who all share the same thinking way of communicating. But not all men who communicate with thinking do so in the same way.

For example, even though both Ted (ESTJ) and Sheldon (ENTJ) are extraverted thinkers, the way they use their thinking is very different. As extraverts, both Ted and Sheldon use their thinking processes in relation to the outer world. They enjoy organizing it, running it, and administering it with efficiency. Where they differ is that Ted uses thinking in relation to sensation (ST)—that is, in regard to facts themselves. Because of his preference for sensation, he enjoys manipulating facts, arranging them, and making sense of them in their own right. Abstract ideas as they relate to thinking are less important to him. This is probably why the ST nucleus is overwhelmingly common in accountants. It is also why Ted is labeled as a Thinker, rather than an Idea Man.

On the other hand, Sheldon's thinking is in the service of intuition (NT). He is not interested in using logical analysis to arrive at the facts themselves, but rather to see how these facts serve the purpose of discovering new possibilities, new enterprises, or new and novel ways of approaching the ordinary. So for Sheldon, abstract ideas are extremely important, but individual details much less so. This is why NT is so frequently found to be the core type of abstract thinkers like scientists, philosophers, and mathematicians. I think of the NT group as the Idea Men because the abstract thinking of the NTs contrasts so strongly with the concrete, detailed thinking of the STs. The classification differs between the Thinkers and the Idea Men only because we can identify these men more by *what* they do than how they talk about it.

Richard (ISTJ) and Alexander (INTJ) are introverts who use the thinking communication style, but because one is a Thinker and the other an Idea Man, they do so differently. The difference between them revolves around their different perceiving styles. Richard somewhat resembles Ted because he uses his thinking to communicate, and his inner life is dominated by sensation. So, like Ted, he is practical and factual. He is interested in applying his factual information to concrete realities.

Alexander uses thinking to communicate, but his inner life is dominated by intuition. The combination makes him somewhat similar to Sheldon, but he uses his abstract thinking skills in a more individualistic way. And because Alexander, unlike Richard, uses intuition rather than sensation as a perceiving style, he is less interested in concrete reality than he is in possibilities. This makes him more innovative, even ingenious, in the ways he seeks to find applications for his creative ideas.

The two TPs, Paul (ENTP) and Cal (INTP), communicate most often through intuition. Their communication style conveys their interests in discussing and developing original, workable ideas. Their only apparent difference is in introversion-extraversion, but as we will see later this seemingly minor alteration of their type creates a major difference in their personalities.

RELATIONAL STYLE OF NTs

With NT at their core, the Idea Men are innovative thinkers and communicate their creative ideas with impersonal logic. They can seem like intellectual narcissists who banter their ideas about with such precision that they come across as insensitive know-it-all types. Their lack of developed feeling contributes to their disregard for the feelings and thoughts of others. With some development of tact, they can be articulate, inspiring teachers.

NTPs' relationships can be more experimental than traditional. NTJs, however, often tend more to develop more traditional relationships. Compared to STs, NTs view relationships more optimistically, less concretely, and as a source of mutually inspired ideas of how to be and where to go. They value subtle indications of commitment over more obvious and concrete signs of care. They value change as an integral part of relating, and want partners to be inspiring and challenging.

SHELDON: AN EXTRAVERTED THINKING TYPE: ENTJ

As an ENTJ, Sheldon also has extraverted thinking but has intuition in place of the sensation of Ted's type (ESTJ). So while Sheldon is also an extraverted thinking type with judging, his auxiliary function is introverted intuition. Because of this, he is much more interested in the possibilities that are related to the facts rather than just the facts in themselves. Sheldon's outgoing nature was obvious to everyone very early in his life. He was a free-spirited child who had to understand the reasons for everything, especially orders from his parents. His natural and insatiable curiosity was a joy to his parents who, as extraverted thinkers themselves, had no trouble reinforcing his inquisitiveness.

Sheldon is a natural leader, respected for his competency, efficiency, and innovative ways of accomplishing what he sets out to do. He is a master of the total picture. He is the school administrator where Ted's son Teddy attends school.

When Teddy's teacher Phil (ESFJ) reported that Teddy was having problems paying attention and getting his work done on time, his father was asked to come to school for a meeting. The meeting proved to be tense for both Phil and Ted. Because he was dissatisfied with Phil's recommendations, Ted went to see Sheldon. Ted wanted to see if there was something more specific that could be done to ensure Teddy's progress.

Instead of discussing his perceptions of Teddy's problem first, Sheldon immediately reacted from the position that, while there was no school policy that would allow Teddy to receive more help than he was already getting in the classroom, perhaps there were some other areas of Teddy's performance in need of investigation. But he was also interested in finding another source of help for Teddy, whom he understood to be an otherwise bright student who was having an inexplicably difficult time.

Sheldon likes to be in control and often has a "take charge" attitude. He is action-, goal-, and task-oriented. His impersonal logic as well as his need for efficiency make him want to explore other possibilities of resolving a problem. Ted's complaint was also a threat to Sheldon's pride and competence; he felt challenged to come up with the best possible workable solution quickly. He feels a strong personal identification with his role as administrator; much of his sense of self-worth comes from being able to feel that he is consistently doing the best possible job. He also feels confidence in the educational system and thinks all problems within it are ultimately solvable. Often to his dismay, this takes more time than he feels it should.

After listening to all the facts that Ted presented, Sheldon suggested that Teddy first be sent to a neuropsychologist to be evaluated for a possible learning disability. If Teddy showed a clear learning disability, there were special education services that could be made available to him.

As extraverted thinkers, neither Ted and Sheldon care for what they perceive as inefficiency or sloppy thinking in others. Since Ted and Sheldon also share the same less-developed feeling function, neither thought that Phil's more feeling approach to Teddy's problem was very practical or workable. And, owing to their inferior introverted feeling, neither of them put much stock in an emotional problem as an explanation for Teddy's difficulty, even though they both gave superficial lip service to the idea.

And since Ted and Sheldon tend to be more critical than supportive in interpersonal relations, to both of them an extraverted feeling type such as Teddy's teacher Phil looks like someone with good intentions who is rather incompetent. Because they are so goal-oriented and analytical, both Ted and Sheldon put getting things done above all else, sometimes even at the cost of stepping on others' toes in the process.

Extraverted thinkers like Ted and Sheldon have relational styles that stress tough-mindedness, organization, and a quick analytical approach to problems. They like to be fair but they can both be impatient with others when things don't go their way. Because they are so independent and prefer to function autonomously, they may not put much stock in the opinions of others, either.

THE ENTJ PROTOTYPE (5%)

Thinking → Intuition → Sensation → Feeling

The ENTJ is an articulate, bold, extraverted thinking type, in many ways similar to the ESTJ. ENTJs are energetic, ambitious, driven, and tough-minded. They are robust and aggressive in getting things done both at work and at home.

In their professional life, ENTJs often seek positions of power through action, and they are extremely result- and goal-oriented. Successful ENTJs often have the appearance and air of the "golden boy," who seems to create endless opportunities and possibilities for rising to the peak of his abilities.

ENTJs tend to be tightly structured and scheduled. They

run on the principle of efficiency, with standard rules for how business, mind, and home are to operate. Along with their ESTJ counterparts, they are among the most competitive of all the types. Theirs is a naturally articulate and persuasive leadership style. Because of this, they have an unusual ability to inspire and encourage others to follow their lead in almost anything they do.

Intellectually, ENTJs are logical, clear-minded, objective, analytical, quick-witted, and decisive. They are masters of the global and comprehensive perspective. They enjoy mental abstractions; complex problems are their forte. Because of this, they are the consummate masters of strategies and planning. They can devise workable tactics for most any situation or problem that captivates their interest. They rise to challenges and are seemingly inexhaustible in their efforts to get things done.

ENTJs also have a unique ability to see many sides and nuances of problems, as well as the ability to devise efficient blueprints for implementing their multisided visions of what needs to be done. Long-range planning is part of their overall perspective, so they are likely to account for down-the-road contingencies.

Interpersonally, ENTJs are autonomous, challenging, self-confident, controlling, and argumentative. Since their relational style is through thinking, they can be emotionally withholding, cool, and even indifferent. Others are often surprised to find they have a gregarious and fun-loving side, because it is difficult for them to relax enough to "let their hair down."

As fathers, ENTJs lead a very active lifestyle with their children, leaning toward activities that stimulate and interest them. They can become bored quickly if their activities don't have at least some element of challenge. If their children don't understand and accept their father's need for constant diversity and challenge, they will rebel or take a compensatory stance in relation to him. Because of their tendency to get so caught up in themselves and their ideas, ENTJ fathers need to develop the capacity to appreciate and value others for their ideas and contributions.

ENTJ fathers emphasize honesty, fairness, and straight-forwardness in family life. They value the need for their partners and children to improve and develop themselves and their unique talents. They not only challenge themselves, they challenge their children as well. When their own need for self-improvement misses the standard they set for themselves, they can become disheartened and depressed. And when things don't go the way they've planned or expected them to, they become even more self-critical and impatient with themselves.

Another aspect of their downside is that when ENTJs don't soften or modify their take-charge, controlling attitude, they can become compulsive and rigid. If they become too preoccupied with their visions, they may lose, ignore, or fail to consider the more subtle details. When this happens, others may find them to be self-righteous and arrogant.

Since ENTJs are so self-critical and it is so difficult for them to relax, they may tend to drive themselves too hard. Like the ESTJs, if they don't know how much is "good enough," they may drive themselves into psychosomatic problems in their attempts to reach unreasonable levels of success.

Because their relational style is through thinking, ENTJs may not have developed their own feeling-based values. When this is the case, they will also ignore the more feeling-based values of others around them, especially those of the feeling types. When they ignore or suppress their own feelings, they are likely to be become complainers or whiners who are moody and inconsolate. ENTJs who suppress their feelings al-together are likely to have outbursts of inappropriate anger, temper tantrums, or seemingly inexplicable moods and depressions.

FREQUENT OCCUPATIONS OF ENTJs

Educational administrator	Computer specialist
Health and education	Mortgage broker
consultant	Biological scientist
Marketer	Systems analyst
Lawyer	Psychologist
Business manager	

ALEXANDER: AN INTROVERTED INTUITIVE TYPE: INTJ

Sheldon referred Teddy to Alexander, a neuropsychologist who is an INTJ. Here we see another major type change based solely on a difference in attitude. Compared to Sheldon (ENTJ), Alexander is much quieter, more low-key, and more interested in his own theoretical approach to specific problems. He has his own highly individualistic opinion on how to think about the world and its problems. Alexander's dominant function is introverted intuition and his auxiliary function is extraverted thinking. As a child he was individualistic and so imaginative that he provided his own sources of stimulation from an already active inner life.

Alexander has had an interest in neuropsychology for many years. He has worked out his own theories and attitudes about problems such as minimal brain dysfunction. His point of view runs counter to much of the traditional medical approach to the diagnosis of brain dysfunction that results from injuries to the brain. While he is very cooperative with his medical colleagues, he considers many of their approaches to this very specialized problem to be superficial and unrealistically simple.

As a forensic psychologist, Alexander is often asked to give his opinion in personal injury cases in which there is a disagreement or confusion about whether the claimant has in fact been brain-injured by an accident. He puts great stock in the diagnostic instruments he uses to evaluate brain dysfunction. He considers their capacity to detect defects in brain function to be sensitive and accurate. He takes even greater pride in his interpretive skills in analyzing the results those instruments produce. In evaluating his patients he understands that even minor brain defects result in extensive effects on behavior and personality.

As an introverted intuitive, Alexander is highly individualistic and independent. While he is interested in possibilities, he was not impressed by either Sheldon's or Ted's obviously authoritative approach to Teddy's problem. In fact, in his interview, Ted's authoritarian attitude stood out so much that Alexander was somewhat put off by it. But giving Ted the benefit of the doubt, he reasoned that Ted might have been put a little on the defensive by Alexander's own insinuation that Teddy might have an intellectual deficit of some kind.

Alexander's auxiliary function, extraverted thinking, corresponds to both Ted and Sheldon's dominant function, so he too is quite well organized and logical. Like Ted and Sheldon, his communication style is thinking, even though he is an introvert. The three of them have a common communication style based on analytical reasoning, logic, and impersonal judgment. All of them were communicating about a problem that seemed to involve the objective evaluation of Teddy's mental capacities. Since all of them were interested in an objective approach in getting to the source of Teddy's school problem, communication among them was fairly straightforward. As a result—barring individual prejudices and idiosyncrasies—they could all communicate fairly easily about this.

Alexander can be somewhat authoritarian in his own right, but he is less conspicuous about it. He puts most confidence in his own authority as well as his own theories, methods, and approaches to assessing what the problem might be. He can be critical of others if they seem to not want to at least look at things from his point of view. Being so individualistic, he often has a tendency to put little stock in the opinions of those who disagree with him. However, he is much more tolerant of the diverging views of people who are close to him.

As part of his assessment, Alexander gave Teddy a series of tests, some to evaluate his intelligence and others to determine if he had a learning disability or an impairment of brain function. Any of these deficits would cause him to have problems paying attention at school. He also gave him some projective tests to see if there was an emotional contribution to his learning difficulty.

Alexander did not find Teddy suffered from any intellectual shortcomings, nor was there a neuropsychological problem involving any kind of mental deficit. In fact, Teddy's IQ was higher than average. Being so certain of his diagnosis, Alexander insisted that Ted would have to explore the possibility of an emotional source of Teddy's problem. He did find some indications from the projective tests that Teddy was lacking in self-esteem and self-worth.

Ted respected Alexander's thorough and meticulous assessment of Teddy as well as the way he presented and discussed the results of the psychodiagnostic tests with him. But he still found Alexander's suggestion to look into an emotional basis for the problem a little difficult to accept. He thought that what Teddy needed most was more concrete information about the world. Also, now knowing Teddy's intelligence was intact, he felt this information further supported his idea that Teddy just needed to try harder by simply putting more effort into his studies.

However, Alexander emphasized that while Teddy's intelligence was perfectly normal, he was not unlike other young boys of his type who were apt to learn more readily when they could understand practical applications of their studies. He also pointed out that boys with temperaments like Teddy's often did not do well in traditionally academic schools or with theoretical subjects. He suggested that Teddy might find school more interesting if his teacher could find a more practical and concrete approach for presenting those things that Teddy needed to learn—perhaps one that would appeal to Teddy's love of animals—rather than trying only to engage him with abstract and unrelated concepts. He further explained that boys of Teddy's type were also more likely to have psychological problems when they had difficulty measuring up to their more academically oriented peers.

Ted was impressed with all the information that Alexander gleaned from these objective tests, as well as by his command of this specialized information and his methodical presentation of it. By using the facts, Alexander was able to get Ted, albeit reluctantly, to finally agree to look into the possibility of an emotional component to Teddy's difficulty. He was able to convince Ted through factual reasoning that emotional factors are quite capable of disrupting a student's ability to perform.

In his explanations and suggestions, Alexander was using his auxiliary function to communicate with Ted. In this way, he appealed to Ted's dominant way of understanding, which is extraverted thinking. In communicating this way, both of them were relating by using a communication style based on thinking.

THE INTJ PROTOTYPE (4%)

Intuition → Thinking → Feeling → Sensation

The INTJ is the most independent of all the types. He is the outstanding individualist who believes deeply in the truth of his own ideas and intuition.

Intellectually, INTJs are among the most rigorous and exacting in their thinking. They demand a lot from themselves and they expect others to have clear and well-reasoned thinking processes. The life of the mind is as important to them as anything else; their internal standards of intellectual excellence are hard to match. Once they have worked out their own ideas they are difficult to convince otherwise.

INTJs are some of the most highly educated of the types; the abundance of advanced degrees found among them attests to their respect for education. Academia is second nature for them, and they will go to great trouble to make sure they get the necessary education. In school, they are often the recognized high achievers with broad academic interests.

Professionally, INTJs are diligent. They are self-paced, and it would be unusual for them to need to be reminded of their duties and responsibilities, because their own standards often exceed the expectations coming from outside. Being so individualistic, they have a natural distaste for bureaucracy and authority. They prefer to do things their own way, though they are often traditional enough that they don't make waves.

INTJs set their sights on inner visions that represent the way they believe it ought to be, often in spite of what others may think. Once they start on a project or idea, they are energetic and persistent in following through, and often difficult to dissuade.

Interpersonally, INTJs are reserved, serious, emotionally cool, and sometimes frugal. They socialize with only a few close friends and what time they spend socially is typically carefully planned and allotted.

INTJ fathers are often very loyal and traditional. They enjoy family life, especially when its festive rituals remain low-key, intimate, and private. They indulge and encourage their children's interests and goals, but are not beyond questioning them if they feel their ideas are not well thought-out. They emphasize the need for their children to adapt and cope with a world they perceive as exciting, yet demanding, and fraught with intellectual and practical challenges to be overcome—all for the purpose of achieving maximum self-sufficiency and the highest level of personal competency.

On the downside, INTJs can be pedantic, rigid, and difficult to convince of another viewpoint. When INTJs become overly preoccupied with their own ideas, they may cut themselves off from creative spontaneity. If they become overly absorbed in their own interests, they can start to withdraw from others. A major problem for them is in becoming too single-minded.

FREQUENT OCCUPATIONS OF INTJs

Psychologist	Chemical engineer
Scientist	Electrical engineer
Life and physical scientist	University professor
Social scientist	Photographer
Researcher	Attorney
Research manager	Attorney administrator
Computer systems analyst	Judge

CAL: AN INTROVERTED THINKING TYPE: INTP

Like Harry, the building repairman (ISTP), Ted's brother Cal is also an introverted thinker. His dominant function is introverted thinking and his auxiliary is extraverted intuition. But unlike Harry (with an ST nucleus) who is more interested in the practical applications of things and information, Cal (with an NT nucleus) is concerned with theoretical ideas and their possibilities, because he relies on his intuition. As a mathematician and professor, Cal is most comfortable and competent when he is immersed in the proof of a new theory. He is somewhat of a loner and, like his nephew Teddy, not easily understood. Because of his perceiving orientation to the outer world, Cal relies on his intuition. In this way he differs from Alexander (INTJ), who because of his judging orientation, relies more on thinking.

Even as a child, Cal alternated between being either very shy or terribly argumentative. He was questioning, inquisitive, and even challenging of his elders. He seemed to enjoy his own thoughts even more than the company of his friends. As a youngster, he was already a voracious reader; reading science fiction, fantasy, and mysteries became an early form of self-amusement. He seemed to enjoy learning for the sake of learning.

Since Cal's auxiliary function is extraverted intuition, the world of ideas and theories provides an endless fascination for his intellect. Although he, like Ted, has a rather undeveloped feeling function, he generally appears less "uptight" and rigid than his brother.

When it comes to himself, Cal can be self-critical and demanding, spending tremendous amounts of time trying to cover all the theoretical bases of his intellectual interests. On the other hand, he is open-minded and accepting of the way Teddy is. He encourages Ted to give Teddy more space, to let him develop in his own way. Though he doesn't say so, Ted thinks Cal's advice is irresponsible, and that it follows from his overly theoretical preoccupations and his lack of "responsible involvement" in a family life. Much to Ted's disapproval, Cal has been divorced for several years and has a son who lives with him.

Since Cal's most undeveloped function is extraverted feeling, he has great difficulty in relationships, particularly romantic ones. As an example of this, Ted cynically recalls the time that Cal fell madly in love with one of his students, whom he idealized beyond reality. According to Ted, he failed to see that she was simply a young girl infatuated with her professor's brilliance and flattered by his interest in her. We will return to this problem of Cal's in chapter 6.

THE INTP PROTOTYPE (5%)

Thinking → Intuition → Sensation → Feeling

The INTP is the most intellectually impressive of all of the types. Like the proverbial absent-minded professor, he is independent and self-determined, with an extraordinary grasp of both thought and language.

Intellectually, the INTPs are curious, logical, creative, and original thinkers whose *raison d'être* seems to be to organize thoughts and concepts. Because their approach is speculative and theoretical, they leave the organization of the outside world of activities and people to others. They enjoy the examination of universal truths and principles. Their cognitive style is marked by ingenuity, cleverness, and logical purity. As nonconformist thinkers, they enjoy discussing and solving complex problems, building conceptual models, and developing unusual and complex ideas. Unlike STs, NTs are oriented to principles rather than facts. They place a strong value on education and are relentless, lifelong learners.

Since extraverted feeling is likely to be their most undeveloped function, they often appear to be emotionally reserved, if not detached. They are often indifferent to others' opinions. They abhor small talk and may appear indifferent to all but those who know them well. Because of this, INTPs are often emotionally aloof and skeptical. They are not infrequently loners.

Professionally, INTPs require work that provides a constant challenge to their creative intellects. Once they have demonstrated to themselves that they have mastered a concept, they proceed to the next challenge. Any project can be challenging to them if it involves an intellectual process. Compared to most of the ST Thinkers, INTPs focus on intellectual processes themselves, rather than on the results or outcomes of those processes.

In their work, INTPs may not have an easy time getting along with others because their intellectual expansiveness requires a lot of tolerance from others and a lot of freedom for themselves. They are intellectually challenging to others and put little stock in established opinions.

They dislike hierarchy, often ignore routine, and dislike the ordinary, especially standard operating procedures. Their best performance occurs in a flexible, unstructured environment in which they can set their own pace and goals. They are some of the most self-determined of all types of men. They are self-directed, self-correcting, and pride themselves on self-mastery. Their personal sense of competency comes from a successful search for conceptually perfect, flawless solutions, in short, in achieving intellectual perfection.

As fathers, INTPs are commonly patient and accepting.

Of paramount importance to them is fostering the growth of their children's intellectual independence. The INTP father doesn't demand or impose but rather *proposes* alternatives for their children. Because of his live-and-let-live attitude, he can sometimes seem passive, indirect, and preoccupied. He pursues hobbies with the same determination as work. Any intellectual process, whether in work or pastime, involves his total concentration and attention.

On the downside, INTPs can be their own worst, fault-finding critics. To others, they may appear to care more about the nature of their projects than they do about people. Without intellectual restraint, they may become so caught in objective analysis that they lose the trees for the forest.

The INTP's need for time alone, quiet, and inner activities may become more important than people. If he fails to find the necessary outlets for his conceptual abilities, he may become cynical or depressed. He may become an irksome, solitary taskmaster who loses sight of the personal dimension of his work.

By overemphasizing his intellectual life, the INTP may fail to develop social skills and family relationships. And without adequate emotional satisfaction and satisfactory relationships he can become overly sentimental, hypersensitive, and overreactive.

FREQUENT OCCUPATIONS OF INTPs

Professor of mathematics, science, economics, or philosophy	Computer programmer
	Computer systems analyst
	Lawyer
Researcher	Photographer
University professor	Psychologist
Biologist	Surveyor
Chemist	Writer

PAUL: AN EXTRAVERTED INTUITIVE TYPE: ENTP

Cal's son Paul is an ENTP. He provides an interesting contrast to his father even though the only apparent typological difference between them is that Cal is an introvert and his son is an extravert. Paul is more animated and lively than his father, and he is constantly on the lookout for new ways of doing routine things. Paul's dominant function is extraverted intuition. And his auxiliary function is introverted thinking. Because Cal's auxiliary function is extraverted intuition, he shares Paul's communication style as well as his interest in novel alternatives of ways to get things done. However, Cal sometimes sees his son as being unusually unfocused and preoccupied with too many possibilities.

In his own childhood, Cal was much more withdrawn than his son is now. So Paul's extraversion and activity level seem comparatively extreme to him. Paul's childhood seemed like a constant scramble for Cal to physically and mentally keep up with him. Continually on the go, Paul was a consistent challenger of any limitations placed on his freedom. Restrictions on him just seemed to make him push back even harder.

Ted, the ESTJ, is Paul's uncle. He often sees his nephew as wild and out of control, which gives him little confidence in Cal's advice about Teddy. Ted reasons that if Cal can't control Paul, he certainly has no place advising him about Teddy. On the other hand, Paul's view of his Uncle Ted is that he has been coopted by the establishment and sold himself out to the system. He sees Ted as another bureaucrat with a narrow vision of how organizations should be run.

Paul has developed a reputation for being a radical within the social welfare system, in which as a social worker he applies his innovative ideas. Paul has a fundamental disrespect for most large organizations and bureaucracies and sees them as inefficient as well as short-sighted. In the day-to-day activities of his job, he is reluctant to follow standard procedures, dislikes rules, and looks for more creative ways to deal with routine. His attitude often puts him at risk with his superiors.

Paul's personal goal is to reform the entire social welfare system with his own global ideas of how it should be run. To others he sometimes seems more intent on outwitting the system than changing it. As an iconoclast and a tough individualist, his ideas are more concerned with restructuring the social welfare system than with the direct benefits to welfare recipients.

Because he is so disconnected from his own feeling values, his extremist ideas don't always consider the impact on those who matter the most. But according to his way of thinking, only when the system itself is adequately restructured will there be any benefit to the recipients. Paul's interest is also often focused on the personalities of the administrators of that system, and he has a genuine aim to understand them. But he sees them as having a blocking effect on his ideas rather than as being supportive of him. He resents being confined by inefficient departmental guidelines and thinks they restrict implementation of more important, relevant, and functional ideas. What is less obvious to him is own impact on the system. As a radical, he would just as soon burn the whole system down and start fresh.

Paul's sense of self-esteem comes from developing a strong sense of personal competency. His eloquence and persuasive point of view, for example, often incite his peers to action.

Unlike his Uncle Ted, Paul's father believes that his head

is in the right place but that he tends to bite off more than he can chew.

THE ENTP PROTOTYPE (6%)

Intuition → Thinking → Feeling → Sensation

The ENTP male is enterprising, ingenious, and ambitious. He is energetic, enthusiastic, outgoing, and often fun to be around. While the ENTP is gregarious, he is also quite independent. ENTPs can be competitive, challenging, and objective in their approach.

In their professions, ENTPs are entrepreneurial, resourceful, and persuasive instigators of change. They are capable of devising creative, foresightful strategies to analyze and deal with complex ideas and projects. Their approach is adaptive, pragmatic, and often quite original. They are capable of accurately and realistically assessing the future implications of their ideas.

ENTPs' greatest difficulty in work life is that they dislike routine, standardized procedures, and rules and regulations. This frequently makes them seek fresh, untried ways of getting things done.

Intellectually, ENTPs have a natural flair for analyzing and organizing complicated mental concepts wholistically. They have a natural tolerance for the complex, and even like it. Flexibility and openness allow them access to many possible ways of expressing and refining ideas. They most like ideas that work and have practical applications. Like the ENTJ, this intellectual openness frequently results in their becoming masters of the larger picture, but they are even less concerned about details than the ENTJ. Much of their competency is derived from developing personal skill in many different areas.

Interpersonally, ENTPs can be enthusiastic, easygoing,

good-humored, and loquacious conversationalists. Their articulate and compelling style gives them the ability to mobilize and inspire others. They can be clever and imaginative in their dealings with others, often rising to positions of leadership because of their novel and convincing points of view.

But when ENTPs become overly preoccupied with their ideas, there is often an impersonal quality in the way they relate to others. This can create a feeling of emotional distance and superficiality in their relationships.

As fathers, ENTPs are easy to please, and very accepting of their children. They don't usually place unfair or unrealistic expectations on them. They commonly have many hobbies and there are varied projects going on around their homes. They are constantly on the lookout for new things to do with their families and are excellent improvisors when things become dull.

Since ENTPs place such a high value on intellectual individualism, they readily support the development of their children's special abilities and skills. They enjoy being good providers for their families, and one of the ways they provide is by supporting their children's interests.

However, ENTPs are usually not as consistent in providing emotional nurturance as their families want them to be. To their families they sometimes seem to be either "off" or "on," alternating between optimistic, enthusiastic participation and self-absorbed detachment. In this way, they can also be experienced as emotionally undependable.

As one of the most occupationally versatile of the types, there are many different professional niches into which ENTPs can comfortably fit. ENTPs' comfort in a wide variety of occupations is limited only by their intolerance and dislike of routine and bureaucracy. Professions with too much routine, too many rules and regulations, and frequent deadlines only serve to frustrate their penchant for freedom in the service of mental abstractions.

The downside of ENTPs is that they can become overly focused on their vision of how things should be to the exclusion of the details of how they actually are. When they don't sufficiently account for details or put enough effort into careful preparation for their complex pursuits, they may end up ill-prepared for the tasks they tackle.

ENTPs can become outspoken, nonconforming iconoclasts who are compelled to see and do things their own way. If their opposition to the status quo becomes too extreme, it may result in their being seen only as oppositional gadflies. If that stance is not modified others may then perceive them as self-righteous, and "above it all."

FREQUENT OCCUPATIONS OF ENTPs

Salesman	Psychiatrist
Photographer	Public relations officer
Computer systems analyst	Actor
Chemical engineer	Journalist
Credit investigator	

SUMMARY OF THE NT GROUP

The way in which NTs perceive is through abstractions and possibilities; the way in which they judge these abstractions is through thinking, that is, through a relatively impersonal decision-making process. For the NTs, theorizing is an important dimension of their quest to understand the world, which they perceive as a largely objective experience. They seek to understand the underlying principles that are at work in the world in which they live. And unlike the Thinkers (STs), they value facts only as evidence or examples of theory and not for their own sake.

As a group, NTs are often self-critical and intellectually perfectionistic. At the same time, they demand that others live up to their high expectations and levels of performance. They show a strong propensity for both ingenuity and a logical grasp of their subject matter. They function best in technical, scientific, administrative, and financial occupations. While they may be ingenious innovators, they often need to balance their ideas with more emotionally harmonious attitudes in the area of human relationships.

For the NT men, relationships seem almost secondary to their desire to understand the "whys" of the world. They can be creative and innovative thinkers and can contribute a great deal in terms of new and unexplored aspects of intellectual life. But they are the "slow learners" in the realm of human relationships.

Having added these descriptions of the NT Idea Men to the ST Thinkers, we have accounted for over 60 percent of men—those in whom the thinking component exists in combination with either sensation and intuition, where it is either the dominant or auxiliary function. We can see that the presence of the thinking function continues to impart a decidedly masculine bent to both the ST and NT groups.

Now we look at the third group, the Doers. These are the sensation-feeling type men in whom thinking is no longer either the dominant or auxiliary function, but at best, the tertiary function or the inferior function. The weakness of the thinking function and the primacy of the feeling function imparts a very different quality to these men's personalities.

CHAPTER 5

The Doers: Phil, Wally, Brian, and Teddy

FREQUENCY OF THE DOERS: 26%

In the United States, and perhaps in the Western world, SFs are more often women than men; they represent almost half of all women. (See table 4 in the appendix.) Twenty-six percent of men are like Brian, Teddy, Phil, and Wally, who belong to the sensation-feeling, or SF, group.

Like the ST group, the SF group uses sensation as their means of perception, but because their judging function is feeling instead of thinking, they differ greatly from the Thinkers. Their most distinguishing characteristic is that they are a very people-oriented group. All of them have some measure of heightened feeling and sensation; and all of them have undeveloped thinking and intuition.

Doers prefer the practical, sensible, concrete, and down-to-earth. For this reason, Doers are rarely impressed by abstract principles. They tend to be realistic in their approach to problem solving rather than allowing themselves to be bound to rules. As pragmatists, they are more likely to find creative ways to use rules than to simply follow them.

AN OVERVIEW OF THE SFs

I have chosen to call sfs the Doers because as a group they are most often attracted to occupations in which their feeling function has some practical application. For this reason, they frequently make wonderful doctors, nurses, and parents.

The characters in the vignettes of this chapter are Brian, an ISFJ, who is Ted's family physician; Phil, an ESFJ, who is Teddy's teacher; Teddy, Ted's son, an ISFP; and Wally, an ESFP, the owner of the stables where Teddy rides. See table 10 in appendix 1 for a summary of each man's dominant and auxiliary function and communication style. As in the previous chapters, the description of each of these character types will be followed by a prototype that will describe the type's more general characteristics.

Of the four types I have called the Doers, two of them, Phil and Wally, are extraverts; Phil is an extraverted feeling type and Wally is an extraverted sensation type. The extraverts, Phil and Wally, tend to be tolerant and easygoing, and are good mediators. They often are skilled at organizational development. They have an extensive capacity to enjoy life; they savor food, possessions, and even tools.

The other two sfs, Brian and Teddy, are introverts. Brian is an introverted sensation type, and Teddy is an introverted feeling type. Teddy and Brian are the introverted pragmatists. They are dependable, responsible, and exquisitely sensitive to details. They are good at jobs that require fastidious attention to specifics and perseverance. Their persistence and problem-solving ability gives them a sense of competence and self-esteem.

We can see from this that while I call the SF group the Doers, there is actually one extraverted feeling type, Phil, and an introverted feeling type, Teddy, as well as an extraverted sensation type, Wally, and an introverted sensation type, Brian. So the group consists of two sensation types and two feeling types.

Again, as in the case of the STs and NTs of the preceding chapters, what all of the men in this group "do best" is related to the nucleus of their type, SF, more than just by their designated type names. All of the SFs have some measure of heightened sensation and feeling, and as a consequence of that, some measure of undeveloped intuition and thinking as well. But the ways in which each of them uses their feeling is different. They all prefer to use feeling processes in combination with sensation. Their preference is to primarily use sensation as a perceptual process and feeling as an evaluative process. The overall mental process of the SF is summed up in the following description:

> SF people, like ST people, rely primarily on sensing for purposes of perception, but they prefer feeling for purposes of judgment. They too are mainly interested in facts that they can gather directly through the senses, but they approach their decisions with more subjectivity and personal warmth. The subjectivity and warmth comes from their trust of feeling, with its power to weigh how much things matter to themselves and others. They are more interested in facts about people than in facts about things.[1]

So, all of the Doers operate by using sensation as a perceiving function, as do the STs. But used in combination with feeling, sensation imparts a quality to the SF group that is quite different from the ST group. Even though there is an extraverted sensation type and an introverted sensation type in both of the groups, they are all very different from each other.

As we have seen, each function of consciousness also has a particular orientation to time. As we saw in our discussion of the ST group, sensation types' orientation to time is largely to the present. But feeling types' relation to time is predominantly to the past.[2] The SF group is designated as the Doers because the interactive effect of the way they use sensation in connection with feeling results in an orientation toward doing things for or with others. This will become even more clear from the vignettes and prototypes that follow.

COMMUNICATION STYLES OF THE SFs

The two FJS of this group, an extravert, Phil (ESFJ), and an introvert, Brian (ISFJ), communicate largely through feeling. The two SPS, Wally (ESFP), an extravert, and Teddy (ISFP), an introvert, communicate most often through sensation. All four of them use feeling in combination with sensation.

SFs like details, evidence, and facts presented through specific examples to which they can relate in a personal way. SFs often use personal experience to discuss ideas, even when those ideas pertain to factual data. They like discussing facts and evidence, but not when they become overly impersonal. SFs' preferred focus in communication is on relationships, other people, and the pursuit of happiness, harmony, and comfort. They enjoy practical, straightforward discussions mostly for the value of relating, not for making points or winning arguments. They avoid or minimize conversations that are too negative or critical, especially those about others. They can always find realistic examples of the positive qualities about anyone. They are agreeable in conversation and can identify and support the positive points others make. And unlike most men, they like to discuss personal reasons for being in relationships, the details of keeping them, and of finding concrete ways to make them better.

RELATIONAL STYLES OF SFs

SFs prefer sociable, friendly, and straightforward communication conveyed through personally meaningful information. They prefer personalizing conversation over discussing more intellectual or abstract topics. They focus on the positive qualities of friends, children, and partners. They show attention, love, appreciation, and kindness toward others in concrete ways. SFs appreciate being asked about their opinions and feelings, but dislike being criticized for how they feel or their emotional reactions. They take others' opinions and feelings seriously and want to be of direct help.

BRIAN: AN INTROVERTED SENSATION TYPE: ISFJ

Brian, an ISFJ, is a family-practice physician who treats Ted's family. His dominant function is introverted sensation and his auxiliary function is extraverted feeling. So he communicates most easily through feeling. There are not many ISFJs among men. They are often the quiet, warm, responsible, service-oriented types who enjoy providing assistance to others in need. Being retiring and introverted, they are not often found in the limelight. They prefer to operate from behind the scenes, doing their jobs unobtrusively and carefully.

As a child, Brian was quiet, obedient, and spent a good deal of his time alone learning to play the violin. He was intrigued by observing and exploring nature, eager to savor the sights, sounds, and textures of all that he encountered. He was very much a child of the moment, and became deeply absorbed in whatever caught his senses.

Brian has an extremely busy family practice, which he enjoys tremendously. He knows many of his patients well and likes attending to their needs. He also enjoys the practice of medicine because it involves methods and procedures with which he can exercise his careful and painstaking approach to both diagnosis and treatment. He is an excellent diagnostician who enjoys discovering the source or cause of his patient's symptoms by following routine, methodical, and trusted methods of examination and tests. He is a realistic and dependable person and his medical practice provides him with many outlets that suit his need to provide good service and care with tangible, clear results.

As Ted sat in Brian's waiting room, he noticed the subdued warmth of the decor and the soft classical music playing in the background. As far as doctors' offices go, this one was welcoming and nonthreatening. Everything in it seemed entirely appropriate and also conveyed its owner's personality perfectly. On a table in the corner were neatly arranged pamphlets describing various self-help approaches to common medical problems. There were also magazines for both adults and children. On the floor there were several toys for the amusement of the children. Paintings of muted pastoral scenes decorated the walls. There were also several photographs of places in Europe that Brian had visited.

Over the years Ted has grown to appreciate and rely on Brian's relaxed warmth and calm manner, as well as his dutiful, meticulous diagnostic approach. Brian always seems dependable, grounded, reasonable, and unhurried. One of his outstanding qualities is his ability to quietly and astutely observe the details of his patient's manner, posture, and even gesture. He is usually able to draw precise inferences from his observations that are useful in his treatment plan. Because his auxiliary function is extraverted feeling, he is tuned in to others and has a careful, considerate manner in his relationships. Brian is not one to jump to conclusions too quickly, because he knows when he doesn't ground his speculations in concrete reality he may miss the mark or be too negative in his prognosis or outlook.

One of the difficulties Brian has is that he is so devoted to his work that he often doesn't find the time to take care of his own needs for relaxation and leisure. When he is at home, he is a dutiful, devoted husband, careful to attend to the needs of his family and friends.

Ted first consulted Brian fairly early in his career, because of hypertension and a tendency to peptic ulcer disease. Brian was extremely thorough in his examination, applying every possible test in order to properly diagnose Ted's problems. After all the tests had been completed, Brian then personally called Ted, inviting him to come in and discuss the results. Brian explained in detail all of the clinical findings to make sure Ted understood which tests needed to be heeded and which could be ignored.

Brian then questioned Ted regarding his moods, feelings, family life, and job, which he felt might be causing Ted his high level of stress. Then he outlined a treatment program, which included vigorous exercise, diet, and some medication; he also suggested that Ted might want to consult a psychologist for supportive therapy in dealing with the stress of his job and his frustration with his son's poor school performance.

Ted eagerly accepted all but the suggestion for psychological help, reasoning that he was able to figure these things out for himself. Besides that, he felt that psychotherapy was a pretty inexact science and thought that "most shrinks need help themselves."

Brian is as interested in facts as Ted is. But Brian is interested in facts as they relate to *people* rather than as they relate to things. This interest gives Brian a quality of interpersonal warmth, which is more suppressed in Ted. Brian's auxiliary function, extraverted feeling, has a socially conventional and harmonious quality to it that allows him to form easy and compatible relationships with his patients. Brian usually doesn't have many friends but those he does have are very close and trusted friends whom he has had a long time. Phil is one of Brian's oldest friends; he is also Ted's son's teacher.

THE ISFJ PROTOTYPE (4%)

Sensation → Feeling → Thinking → Intuition

The ISFJs are quiet, warm, sincere, and have a genuine desire to help others. They are kind, considerate, and dependable. They like to have comfortable relationships with only a few long-term friends. They are often quite solicitous of others. But while adept at drawing others out, they are quiet, reserved, and serious men who keep themselves in the background. ISFJ men don't usually divulge much about themselves and rarely discuss their personal feelings except with those close to them. They sometimes enjoy group activities if they are with others they know reasonably well. Otherwise they tend to be shy.

The intellectual style of ISFJs is characterized not only by thoroughness, but also by cautious and meticulous attention to details. Their thinking occurs behind a veneer of quietness and calmness. They don't approach a problem without carefully prioritizing. Problem solving involves a diligent regard for what is practical, so they focus on what seems to be the most real and immediate aspect of a problem. They also like to go about that process by themselves with plenty of time for quiet concentration. Only after arriving at what they consider to be the best possible, most correct solution do they include others in their conclusions, presenting the results of their thinking with tact and consideration. They have definite rules and regulations for getting themselves where they want to go. Practical flow sheets, lists, and detailed routines work best for them. They painstakingly focus on what seems most actual. Their learning style is best described by a practical hands-on approach, which allows them to use their natural sensory and kinesthetic awareness.

Professionally, ISFJs enjoy work in which they can be of service work but in which they also accomplish specific tasks. They like jobs requiring dedication to others, especially direct human service that is attentive to people's special needs. Because they are task-oriented and structured toward getting the job done, they prefer to work with things they can see. As quiet providers of assistance they like consistent routines, clear expectations, and want to be sure they know what they are doing. They like to meet requirements and assignments that are clear and tangible, and produce concrete results.

ISFJs like to work alone rather than in groups; time alone seems to enhance their productivity. They rarely need much supervision once they know what is expected of them and what the job itself requires. They have good follow-through and like to organize themselves around what is important to them. It is difficult for them to begin a new project without having the necessary steps worked out in advance so they can set their goals clearly. Disorder, disorganization, and disruptions interfere with their ability to concentrate. They can't work when things are out of order. As employees they are compliant and loyal, honoring existing hierarchies. They are highly self-determined, self-motivated, and proud of all they do, rarely asking others to do what they wouldn't do themselves.

In family life, ISFJs are responsible and traditional. They have uncomplicated, straightforward values: security and loyalty. They like to provide tangible benefits for their families so as to make life as comfortable and trouble-free for them as possible. Their sense of self-worth as parents, partners, and providers is attached to feeling worthy of their families.

ISFJs are devoted, dutiful fathers who are protective of their children and sensitive to their individual needs. Since they are so conscientious, they tend to worry about their partners and children. They are patient, tolerant, and emotionally supportive of both their mates and children.

As partners, ISFJs value stability in marriage and family values and expect their partners to feel likewise. As intimates, they may not verbalize their feelings of love and tenderness directly, but try to express them through thoughtful attention and care to their partner's needs. Their feeling is more tangibly expressed in their collections of momentos, scrapbooks of family events, and material goods they provide the family. Because of their stability, dedication, and devotion to their families, their relationships are frequently long-term. Since they place such a high value on a harmonious family life, they often avoid confrontation, arguments, and conflict.

On the downside, the ISFJ's inferior function is extraverted thinking. As a result he may put off leisure and relaxation, and keep his feelings to himself. He may not develop the ability to see beyond the present and the concrete to future possibilities, as his thinking may become overly preoccupied with so many immediate facts that he loses sight of other implications. If his intuition (tertiary function) is negative, he may imagine the worst outcomes and become overly pessimistic or suspicious. He may focus too much on past negative experience. Being disrespected or disregarded causes the ISFJ to feel deeply hurt.

FREQUENT OCCUPATIONS OF ISFJs

Family-practice physician
Health-service worker
Health technician
Medical technologist
Nurse
Licensed vocational nurse
Speech pathologist
Librarian
Library assistant
Preschool or elementary
school teacher
Teacher's aide
Bookkeeper
Clerical supervisor
Curator
Private household worker
Secretary

PHIL: AN EXTRAVERTED FEELING TYPE: ESFJ

Teddy's teacher Phil is an ESFJ. Phil's childhood was marked by his love of friends, high energy, and an obvious need to try to please everyone around him, especially his parents. He had an unusual sensitivity to others and was often disturbed by others' conflicts, even if they didn't involve him directly. He seemed to be more emotionally vulnerable than other children and was quick to assume blame even when it didn't properly belong to him.

As an extraverted feeling type, Phil is gregarious, open, and warm. His auxiliary function is introverted sensation. As a helpful, compassionate, and nurturing person he makes an ideal teacher. His enthusiasm for teaching and fondness for children make him a favorite of the other teachers at his school. His principal sees him as one of the fairest, most sensitive, and most considerate members of the faculty.

Phil's classroom is always organized, neat, and colorfully

decorated. He believes that children thrive on positive reinforcement and learn best in a supportive, comfortable, and
attractive learning environment. He takes pride in his students' progress and does all he can to make sure they feel
successful in school and good about themselves. He also tries
to understand the individuality of each of his students as
much as possible so that he can better address their unique
concerns and problems. At the same time, he tries to provide
consistent and clear expectations of what is required of them
when they are in the classroom or on the playground.

When "his" kids don't do well Phil sometimes feels that
he may not be doing all that he can to help them—a form of
self-criticism more than an accurate assessment of his efforts.
As a result, Phil felt threatened and insecure by Ted's con-
frontational and challenging style. Phil knew within himself
that he tried very hard to make Teddy's school experience as
rewarding as possible. However, he is sensitive to authority
and often intimidated by the judgments of men in powerful
positions like Ted, who have no reluctance in expressing their
opinions. He is particularly vulnerable to criticism when he
feels it is unfair or unjustified. Ted's manner made him feel
unappreciated, when what he most needs is approval and reassurance.

Some of the difficulties in communication between these
two come from their opposing relational styles: Ted's communication style is through extraverted thinking and Phil's is
through extraverted feeling. And since the nuclei of their types
is in direct opposition, the impact of their relational styles will
be difficult for both of them. Ted's more direct, assertive, logical, objective style contrasts strongly with Phil's more easygoing, subjective, feeling approach. For Phil's taste, Ted is too
much in his head and not understanding enough about either

Teddy or him. For Ted, Phil seems overly sympathetic and not demanding enough.

As we have seen, Ted's type is the most common among men, but Phil's type is the most common among women. There are over twice as many male extraverted thinking types than there are male extraverted feeling types. ESFJ males are something of typological oddballs because they make up only eight percent of the male population. Typologically, they are more like the "average" woman. The warm, accepting, nurturing, and compassionate ESFJ female is virtually the archetype of the traditional mother. ESFJ men are primarily oriented to traditional family values and harmonious relationships. They organize and prioritize their lives around providing service to others. Because of this they are not likely to communicate or relate well to other mainstream men. It is no surprise that Phil usually gets along much better with the mothers of his students than he does with their fathers.

ESFJs are as well organized as their ESTJ counterparts, but their organizational style is directed toward ensuring that the needs of others are met in the most efficient, tangible, and congenial way possible. They also don't like to needlessly waste time, material, or resources but again, this is in the service of ensuring and gratifying the needs of others.

Phil has something in common with Brian, whose auxiliary function is extraverted feeling, in contrast to Ted and Phil's relational styles. Brian has been a friend of Phil's for years and enjoys Phil's frequent barbecues and parties at which Phil is the consummate host. Phil is aware that Brian is Ted's son's doctor; they have spoken appreciatively about Teddy's quiet warmth and his love of animals on several occasions.

THE ESFJ PROTOTYPE (8%)

Feeling → Sensation → Intuition → Thinking

The ESFJ man is outgoing, warm, and compassionate. He enjoys providing for the practical needs of his family and those close to him. Since ESFJ is the most frequent female type, and there are only half the number of men with this type as women, he has some interesting similarities with women of the same type, as well as differences resulting from his socialization as a man. Males who are extraverted in their feeling are as rare among men as extraverted thinking females are rare among women.

ESFJ men have socially appropriate feelings for almost every situation; they have a list of "shoulds" and "should nots" for any occasion. Their responses are helpful, heartfelt, and warm. They frequently idealize people they like, often overlooking faults that are obvious to others. As the consummate hosts they nurture and attend to others' needs in ways that are unusual for most men. Being some of the most obviously well socialized and sensitive of men, they more freely express their appreciation and approval of others and are also equally hurt by indifference and lack of tact. They value appearances, social appropriateness, and social standards. With all of this social hypersensitivity they are prone to overdeveloping their personas, making them socially correct, but with the potential for emotional superficiality.

Since ESFJs need the stimulation provided by social contacts, it is often difficult for them to be alone. If they become isolated, their restlessness will usually force them to reach out to others.

With extraverted feeling as their dominant function, ESFJs are not very academically oriented. They tend to be non-intellectual and nonabstract in their thinking approach. They seem to learn best in structured situations that provide plenty of direct experience.

Professionally, ESFJs are conscientious and responsible. They enjoy service-oriented careers. In carrying out the responsibilities of their jobs, they are orderly, efficient planners who do best in structured situations and organizations. They tend to accept roles in organizations in which they can maintain a personable work style, and they like expectations of them to be clear and consistent.

ESFJs respect hierarchy, authority, and status. Sometimes they may be too deferent to or dependent on authority figures, especially extraverted thinking types. They like their own opinions and decisions to reflect their responsiveness to the needs of others. They are more likely to enjoy decisions when they are applied in useful, helpful ways to people and things. They are often reliable, well-informed, and committed, as well as responsive to others' needs.

Friendly, helpful, and efficient work environments that are also warm allow ESFJs to do their best work—actively meeting the needs of others. Like the ESTJ managers, they value efficiency, time, and resources, but goodwill and the cooperation of others is also reflected in their managerial style. They try to plan, communicate, and make decisions with as much attention to the needs of others as the situation will allow.

The family life of the ESFJ tends to be simple, secure, reliable, and cooperative. They often assume, without being asked, more than their share of family responsibility. More than any other type, extraverted feeling men (and to a lesser extent, ISFJs and INFJs) are the ones who agree be househusbands when their wives want to work outside the home. They may cherish family life so much they are willing to sacrifice outer world achievements for a chance to have greater closeness to their children. (Even among these types, however, accepting such a role demands a sizable sacrifice of their conventional presumptions about masculinity.)

If their own childhoods were happy, ESFJs are often nostalgic about them. They were typically the "good children"—reliable, cooperative, and eager to please their parents. They often report that they enjoyed their early family life.

ESFJs are good at being parents and they like it. They are responsive, sympathetic, accepting, and reliable. As extraverts, they often take on the part of social planner for the family and involve themselves in community and church activities as well. But they like all of these activities to be scheduled and well planned. Leisure is an important part of their family life as well, but their responsibilities to family and home come first.

Relationship itself is primary for ESFJ men. They are more likely than other types of men to marry extraverted feeling women, because they are much more aware of their need to be needed, appreciated, and loved, certainly more so than thinking type men are. Without a steady, ongoing supply of affection, extraverted feeling men quickly need reassurance that everything is all right. "Everything" usually means the feeling level and values of the relationship.

ESFJs are soft-hearted and often sentimental. They enjoy showing their warmth in material ways. Providing "the better things of life" to ensure their partner's and children's comfort is important to them. Unlike many other male types, they are likely to remember, plan for, and celebrate birthdays, anniversaries, and other special occasions. They like their own special events to be recognized as well. If they are not, they are offended and hurt, but because they have been socialized against expressing hurt and vulnerability, they might not say so.

When their own affectional needs are overly strong, ESFJs often marry other needy types and usually stay in the relationship a long time—sometimes too long. When that happens they may be labeled as codependent, because they don't allow their partners to accept responsibility for themselves. As responsible peacekeepers, they often feel betrayed by indifference, accusations of wrongdoing, or by guilt-provoking maneuvers on the part of those close to them. Their self-avowed goal is to keep their relationships harmonious, sometimes at all costs. It is the extraverted feeling father, for example, who often intercedes in conflicts between his wife and children, and urges both of them to be nice to each other and back away from conflict.

As fathers, ESFJs are accepting, attentive, and consistent in their expectations of their children. They expect their children to be obedient and respectful. As pleasers themselves, they expect to be pleased by others, including their children. While the rules they set down for children's behavior are usually clear, they are humanistic and not applied in an arrogant or unfair way. Since they are rule abiders themselves, they expect others to be too. They tend to perceive infractions of family rules as reflecting a lack of loyalty. ESFJ fathers see their children's commitment to family life as a natural responsibility.

The inferior function of the ESFJ is introverted thinking, and his tertiary function is introverted intuition. Therefore on the downside, the ESFJ has a habit of worrying that things won't turn out the way he would like them to. In short, he is often pessimistic because his intuition may be negative and undeveloped.

In addition, ESFJs' keen sensitivity and high standards in relationship may leave them easily hurt when things don't go the way they expect them to. They may become depressed or melancholy if they feel, or think, they are receiving too much blame. Many times they are prepared to blame themselves even before others do. If they *are* the recipients of excessive criticism they can become spiteful and critical themselves, nagging and blaming others for not appreciating "all they have done." Because of their heightened awareness of others' feelings, they may be finely tuned to just how and where to hurt back. Too much of a need for harmony can backfire and cause them to overlook the beginnings of problems that would be better faced early on. Since they have a strong need for good feeling and camaraderie, negative feelings are difficult for them to accept, and even more difficult to handle appropriately. In trying to manage negative feelings they may resort to ignoring or denying that anything is wrong.

ESFJs need to manage anger and conflictual feelings more openly by seeing them as an occasional and necessary part of relating in depth. In trying to please others, they have a tendency to overlook their own needs, thereby becoming even more sensitive to a lack of appreciation. They may take on too many responsibilities for others and shortchange themselves in the process. They need to give more to themselves as well as learn to be more openly accepting of what others do want to offer them. Paradoxically, they have a strong need for approval from others but they have as much trouble accepting praise as criticism and negative feedback. They need to become more assertive about their own needs and more accepting of praise and nurturing from others.

Because of their emotional sensitivity, ESFJs may assume they know others' needs more than others do. If they can't accept the negative feedback that perhaps they are wrong and simply don't know others' needs very well, they may become increasingly difficult for others to be around. In the worst case, ESFJs may become domineering martyrs, bossy, rigid, overly emotional, and irrational.

ESFJs may sometimes need to be a little more impersonal, a little less caught up in details, and look a little further beyond the immediate situation. They may need more options, choices, and alternatives for themselves. If they don't allow themselves alternative ways of perceiving what is available, they will miss the larger picture.

FREQUENT OCCUPATIONS OF ESFJs

Medical secretary	Radiological technician
Receptionist	Religious educator
Dental assistant	Speech pathologist
Nurse	Clergyman
Childcare worker	Hairdresser
Elementary school teacher	Cosmetologist
Home economist	Retail salesperson
Office manager	Restaurant worker
Home management advisor	Healthcare worker

TEDDY: AN INTROVERTED FEELING TYPE: ISFP

Ted's son Teddy, an ISFP, is a quiet and retiring child not always easy to know. As an introverted feeling type, he is reserved in his feelings and not likely to reveal much of what is going on unless one spends a good deal of time finding out. He is a collector of stray animals, the kind of person they naturally follow home. Teddy has a rare warmth, sympathy, and kindness; he would like to be a veterinarian.

However, it seems that Teddy's distraction and difficulty in school might keep him from following his dream. Like others of his type, he is curious but not intellectually or academically oriented, so formal education is difficult to endure, and advanced education could be even less tolerable.

At Brian's suggestion, Phil invited Ted to a conference to discuss Teddy's progress. When Ted arrived, Phil said how much he appreciated Ted's concern and his taking the time to come. He told Ted how much he liked Teddy's sensitivity, modesty, and unassuming nature. But he was concerned about his apparent indifference toward school as well as his poor performance. He explained to Ted that he was confused as to why Teddy wasn't doing better. He had some observations about Teddy that he felt Ted would be interested in hearing. Perhaps after hearing them, Ted might make some suggestions of his own as to how Phil might be more helpful.

Phil assured Ted that Teddy was not disruptive of the classroom, or even outwardly uncooperative. He explained that Teddy had often seemed reticent, even preoccupied at times, and that it was difficult to get him to talk about what was going on with him. Teddy had difficulty attending to the routines of the classroom. He often seemed distracted, seeming to prefer to stare out the window or to draw pictures of animals. He also seemed easily bored, disliked the structure of the classroom, and fussed in his seat if there was a long period of quiet. Teddy also disliked competitiveness and often seemed complacent. Phil had gone out of his way to give Teddy a lot of positive strokes when he did do what was expected of him, but Teddy hadn't responded to this approach.

Listening to Phil, Ted found himself wondering why Phil had so much gushy feeling about Teddy if he wasn't measuring up in the classroom. Ted then told Phil that he thought he was perhaps being overly accommodating, too easy with Teddy. Ted suggested that Phil wasn't pushing him hard enough — maybe Teddy needed more discipline and awareness of consequences to get on the right track. Maybe, he said, Phil should tell Teddy that he would have to stay after school and finish what he wasn't doing in class. Ted, for his part, would try reasoning with Teddy at home about the importance of more "stick-to-itiveness" and his need to pay more attention to the details of his work at school.

Because they are both extraverts, neither Teddy's father nor Phil seemed fully able to understand him. Both of their most available functions (extraverted thinking and extraverted feeling) are quite different from Teddy's dominant introverted feeling and his auxiliary extraverted sensation. Whenever two extraverts sit down to discuss an introvert's problems, especially an introverted feeling type, there are bound to be misunderstandings. Teddy's type is perhaps one of the most easily misunderstood types anyway.

Unlike Teddy, Ted and Phil are judging types. Each of them like things clear, distinct, and decided. Teddy's more spontaneous and nonregimented manner makes him appear to be almost passive-aggressive in his efforts to be his own person and do things at his own pace and in his own time. His father's strong controlling tendencies are in direct conflict with Teddy's need for freedom and his need to try things at his own pace. Teddy's lack of structure and direction is a thorn in his father's side. Ted sees this as a definite shortcoming rather than a difference in temperament.

The relational styles of Ted and Teddy are generally at odds with each other because Ted's communication style is thinking and Teddy's is through sensation. Where Ted is strong, logical, fast, efficient, and directive, Teddy is yielding, slow, pragmatic, and unregulated. Teddy is not the son Ted would have imagined having. The difficulty in their relational styles is exaggerated because Teddy's dominant function, in-

troverted feeling, is his father's inferior function. Ted's introverted feeling causes him to see Teddy as unaggressive and
emotionally soft.

Teddy's type occurs in only 5 percent of men. It is a difficult type for a modern man to be, and even more so for a
boy growing up in a world where the standard for men is
quite the opposite. By conventional standards such a boy's
gentle quietness and lack of intellectual drive make him seem
unmanly and unmotivated.

THE ISFP PROTOTYPE (5%)

Feeling → Sensation → Intuition → Thinking

The ISFP is a man whose quiet sensitivity, low visibility,
and subtlety in expressing himself make him one of the most
difficult types for a man to be. His subdued relational style
makes him one of the most introverted of the introverts. He
goes about his life with little need to influence or control others, rarely imposing himself on situations or other people.

Interpersonally, ISFPs may appear to be almost self-
effacing because they need to blend into any environment in
which they find themselves. As introverted feeling types, they
are not good at expressing themselves emotionally. In addition, although they are warm, quiet, friendly, and unassuming, they may appear to be socially awkward or inhibited.

Professionally, ISFPs often have a strong service orientation. Also, to really enjoy what they do, it has to have practical
significance. Their work must be direct, personally rewarding,
and have a purpose. They may be found in artistic and other
creative endeavors. They can be quiet, unhurried, behind-the-
scenes workers. Too much structure, excessive planning, and
rigidity can block their creative efforts. Since they are non-
competitive and shy about offering their services, they may be

seen as lacking direction and motivation. But their general work style is cooperative, adaptable, and helpful. And whatever they do, they strive to do it well, and in accord with what they believe in.

Intellectually, nontheoretical interests appeal to ISFPs the most. They are keen observers of details and like what is doable. Because they are the most nonacademic of the types, they often avoid formal education. In fact, they drop out of school more often than any of the other types. School subjects that are practical, relevant, and people-oriented appeal to them. They are highly tactile learners and enjoy uncomplicated kinesthetic perception that is exciting to their senses. They like new ways of doing things and can be easily bored by routines. They like unconventional problem solving because it appeals to their need for sensory stimulation more than intellectual understanding. They don't necessarily want to understand the world, they just want to live in it and make a contribution based on their feeling values.

ISFPs like their family life to be active, yet also relaxed and leisurely. Like the ISFJs, they avoid conflict. They are the loyal peacemakers. They enjoy solitary pursuits. When they do socialize, it is with like-minded, easygoing friends who share their values.

As fathers, ISFPs are uncommonly kind, receptive, and helpful with their children. They are nondemanding, nonjudgmental, and sympathetic, but not necessarily empathic. They are curious explorers, with a desire to have their children see and appreciate as much of natural life as they can. They enjoy physical activity, the outdoors, and activities like camping, hiking, and exploring nature. Their own appreciation of nature is straightforward, spontaneous, and unpretentious.

At their best, ISFPs are trusting, sensitive, gentle, and caring with their partners. They express their need for affiliation through activity. They enjoy a life lived harmoniously, quietly, and unobtrusively as possible. Unless they have an unusually perceptive mate, they may be misunderstood even by those closest to them. They are not particularly searching for meaning in life, and they seek recognition based mostly on what they do rather than who they are. Others, especially extraverts, may find them complacent and too easily satisfied with too little. The image of the "lonely cowboy," or Marlboro man, sitting alone, free on the night plains by a fire, sipping his coffee after a hard day of riding and herding provides a good portrait of the ISFP. Today, the life of a forest ranger or environmental activist would also provide an outlet for the ISFP's love of freedom, nature, and animals.

On the downside, if ISFPs become restless and dissatisfied they may also become impulsive, seeking stimulation for the sake of itself. Failure to find creative outlets for themselves may result in their becoming self-critical, unassertive, and nondirect. They may be too easily hurt by others and if that happens they may withdraw in order to insulate and protect themselves. If there are too many demands on them, they may leave projects unfinished, goals for themselves unmet. If their need to blend in becomes too strong they may practically become invisible. If they don't find adequate and meaningful outlets for their interests they can become complacent couch potatoes, resorting to excessive daydreaming or too much television.

FREQUENT OCCUPATIONS OF ISFPs

Licensed vocational nurse	X ray technician
Physical therapist	Carpenter
Nurse	Athlete

Dancer
Dance and movement
  therapist
Bookkeeper
Personal service worker
Personal secretary
Legal secretary
Clerical supervisor

Dental assistant
Medical assistant
Food service worker
Mechanic
Repairer
Storekeeper
Stockclerk

WALLY: AN EXTRAVERTED SENSATION TYPE: ESFP

There *is* one extravert with whom Teddy can relate quite well—Wally, the owner of the stables where Teddy goes horseback riding on the weekends. Wally is an ESFP whose dominant function, extraverted sensation, matches Teddy's auxiliary function. All of their preferences except for introversion-extraversion are the same. Because both their communication styles are through sensation, they each enjoy talking about practical, simple, down-to-earth pleasures.

Wally knows about the difficulties of early school life first-hand. As a youngster he also didn't do well in school and found its routines stale and uninteresting. Although he barely made it into college, he quickly became a beer-drinking fraternity boy and his academic life was cut short soon after it started. Fortunately, he inherited the family stables where he grew up and spent most of his life.

Wally is a friendly, gregarious, and energetic worker at the stables. He works hard, enjoys nature, and likes to be close to animals. He enjoys being in the middle of things, but dislikes the routines involved in running the stables as a business. Everyone at the stables enjoys Wally's easygoing, fun-loving, and boisterous nature. He is quick to share what he knows and tries to include others in all aspects of life around the stables. The stables have been in Wally's family for several generations and Wally likes to think of the business as a pleasurable family affair rather than just a business.

Wally first noticed Teddy quietly admiring a favorite Arabian at the stables one day, and he invited him to take the Arabian out for a ride. Wally could immediately appreciate and understand Teddy's fascination with horses, especially Arabians. He could sense Teddy's excitement and pleasure in being close to nature and horses. He vividly remembered his own enthusiasm as a child in being around horses and working for his father there.

Teddy felt enraptured and exhilarated from riding that beautiful and majestic Arabian. Ever since that day, Wally and Teddy had been fast friends. Together they spend hours around the horses, with Wally showing Teddy the essentials of grooming and sharing his knowledge of Arabians.

In that environment Teddy seems to come to life. Wally's generosity, kindness, and sharing nature put him at ease. He feels accepted by Wally just for who he is. He admires Wally's exquisite attention to every detail of the horses' care. In return, Wally appreciates and shares Teddy's excitement about the Arabians.

The fun at the stables on the weekends makes other parts of Teddy's week feel dull and boring. Returning to school on Mondays seems especially dreary. Here Teddy resumes his seemingly withdrawn state, often drawing pictures of horses at his desk. He *could* be made to do the minimum at school by his father's threat of taking away his riding privileges.

THE ESFP PROTOTYPE (7%)

Sensation → Feeling → Thinking → Intuition

The ESFP is a man who is lively, very energetic, enthusiastic, and fun-loving. More than any of the other types he has an unmatched *joie de vivre.*

ESFPs have sunny, charming, and winsome personalities. They are optimistic, gregarious, playful, spontaneous, and entertaining. As warm and friendly as ESFPs are, they require equal amounts of affirmation and approval from others. They prefer activities that include others in highly compatible ways. Sharing their feelings and experiences with others is not just a favorite pastime, but an ongoing need in their lives. They enjoy actively indulging in others' encounters and adventures as well as having others participate in their own pastimes.

Professionally, ESFPs enjoy working in groups, preferring participative team projects over working in isolation. They are verbally facile, expedient problem solvers. They dislike routine, especially unrelated, recurring procedures.

Because ESFPs are so dominantly extraverted in their sensation, they most often are apt to be nonintellectual and nonacademic. This is not meant to imply that they are less bright, clever, or resourceful than other types. Rather, their intellectual style is characterized by adaptability, simplicity, realism, and practicality. They are rarely interested in knowledge for its own sake, but in what can be done with it, especially in the area of human service. Where they stand out is in their ability to be interpersonally sensitive and keenly observant of others. They learn best when they can feel deeply involved and really enjoy the experience of learning.

With their families, ESFPs are generous and enjoy being active and at the forefront of family life. Spirited and easygoing, they enjoy many activities that involve the whole family.

As fathers, ESFPs are sympathetic, attentive, and helpful to their children. They keep abreast of their children's interests and find direct, ongoing ways to be of service and help. Because they frequently are athletic and enjoy sports themselves, they are likely to be their children's coaches and umpires. They are at their best when they can be leisurely, fun-loving performers for their families.

On the downside, the ESFP may sometimes leave others, especially introverted partners and children, feeling overwhelmed by his hypersocial enthusiasm. His buoyant nature may lead them to see him as a self-indulgent hedonist who lacks restraint and direction.

Because inferior introverted intuition is the weakest function of ESFPs, they may not pay enough attention to possibilities and options for themselves. Extraverted sensation gives them a nonobjective bias, and because emotionally uninspiring activities can bore them, they may resist careful, long-range planning. Their dislike of routine and planning can cause them to end up disorganized and overextended, with numerous unfinished projects.

FREQUENT OCCUPATIONS OF ESFPs

Recreation worker	Receptionist
Coach	Religious educator
Sales representative	Respiratory therapist
Insurance agent	Teacher
Designer	Transportation operative
Childcare worker	Waiter
Clerical supervisor	Library attendant
Factory supervisor	Cashier
Food service worker	

SUMMARY OF THE SF GROUP

With these descriptions of the SF types we have accounted for the sensation component when it exists in combination with feeling as either the dominant or auxiliary function in men's type. Comparing the STs with the SFs, we see that the SFs are better suited to dealing with the *personal* realm—matters that involve weighing the value of things against the analysis of them. SFs' orientation to the world is also factual, but it is largely interpersonal as well. In SFs, the presence of the feeling function in its interaction with sensation creates a departure from the more stereotyped masculine quality of the STs. SFs' communication and relational styles are generally accepted as the more socially appropriate ways for women to communicate than for men. This is particularly true for the extraverted feeling type, of which Phil, the ESFJ, is an example.

As we have seen, this particular combination is preferred by only 26 percent of men. There are twice as many women in the SF group as men. The ESFJ is the most common type among women, and there are over twice as many ESFJ women than men. And among all of the individual SF types, with the exception of ISFP, there are usually distinct differences between men and women; the numbers of ISFP men and women are about equal. As we have seen, the group most unlike the sensation-feelers are the intuitive-thinkers.

As we have seen above, feeling judgments are more pronounced in the extraverted feeling group than they are in the introverted feeling group. Extraverted feeling is much more obvious and on the surface. One doesn't have to guess whether a given man is a feeling type when his feeling function is extraverted.

Introverted feeling males may have deep feeling, but it is rarely on the surface; in fact they may appear cool, distant, or even aloof. Here it is good to remember that "still waters run deep." On the surface neither Eliot nor Teddy appear to have a great deal of feeling judgment compared to Phil, for example, yet it is an integral part of their way of experiencing themselves. To miss their feeling function is to miss an essential part of who they are and how they relate. Since, as introverts, they use their auxiliary function to relate to the outer world, their feeling values are often not obvious to others.

Another important basic difference between the STS and the SFS is reflected in the development of predominant skills within the two groups. Men who prefer thinking and sensation are more skillful at dealing with inanimate objects, machinery, principles, or theories. None of these have any inconsistent and unpredictable feelings, and all of these can be handled objectively and logically. On the other hand, men with sensation and feeling are better skilled in matters involving people and personal values.[3] Men who prefer feeling— whether it is their dominant or auxiliary function—are thus drawn to very different occupations than men who prefer thinking.

When the nucleus of a type includes feeling in combination with sensation rather than thinking, the judging function changes the quality of the SFS' approach to decision making to one that is more subjective than that of the STS'. This addition of the feeling function introduces a greater dimension of interpersonal warmth, one which STS rarely have as a prerogative. So SF males are potentially freer to express caring, sympathy, and warmth in their dealings with others as well as in their work. I say potentially, because they may still be so tied to conventional masculine expectations that they are unable to fully take advantage of all that the feeling function has to offer them.

As we did with the STS, we can break down the male SF

group even more closely by looking at their lifestyle preference, J or P. The J or P factor makes for some wide-ranging
differences between them.

SFJs like Phil and Brian account for 13 percent of men
and differ significantly from their SFP counterparts, Wally and
Teddy, who represent another 13 percent of men. Men with
extraverted feeling and introverted sensation are much more
related to others, owing to the presence of the feeling function. Their fellowship revolves more around social, familial,
sports, and caretaking functions. They are more easygoing,
and their activities are less stringently ritualized than those of
other men. Dealings between them are not as emotionally re-
strictive and include more emotional fellowship, with involvement in lodges, clubs, and sporting events. They are more
likely to indulge the playful, regressive parts of themselves,
even if it is often in ritualized form, such as tailgate parties,
barbecues, and so on.

Emotional responses of SFJ fathers to their sons are likely
to be less critical or demanding, and more overtly positive.
They are freer to give reinforcement and encouragement. SFJs
usually express their appreciation, admiration, and care for
others easily.

SFJs are frequently found in occupations that are traditionally more "feminine" and service oriented. They value
professional accomplishments that involve more direct service
to others. And while they are extremely responsible and dependable, they are not as likely to take their work so seriously
as their ST and NT brothers do.

SFPs are quite different from SFJs because of their perceiving orientation. For example, while Phil and Brian take
more responsibility and structure their lives more thoroughly,
Wally and Teddy are often equally known for their lack
of planning, general disorganization, and lack of follow-

through. They enjoy more freedom, laxity, and relaxation. Generally, SFPs are more adventurous than SFJs. SFPs may not take themselves as seriously as SFJs. Compared to SFJs, SFPs generally like their lives to be more adaptable and flexible. They are less structured and sometimes more impulsive.

A difference between Wally and Teddy in their relationships with others follows mainly from Wally's extraversion and Teddy's introversion. Wally is more gregarious, expressive, and open. Teddy tends to be more reclusive and harder to draw out, so he may seem less sensitive and more preoccupied. Wally is more challenging with others.

SFP fathers are as emotionally supportive with their children as SFJs, and even more inclusive. They seem to worry less about their children than the SFJs.

Having covered the STs, the NTs, and the SFs, we have now discussed about 87 percent of the male population. Now we will turn our attention to the last, and smallest, of the type groups among men, the Dreamers, or the NFs.

CHAPTER 6

The Dreamers: Pablo, Jerry, Dean, and Eliot

FREQUENCY OF THE DREAMERS: 14%

Men who have NF at the core of their type are the smallest of the type groups and represent a relatively small proportion of the male population, almost 14 percent. Compared to the ST group, who make up over 40 percent of men, NFs are truly a minority among men. This underrepresentation makes them feel especially at odds with other men because there are so few of them and also because it is a difficult type for a man to be. As we will see, as a group their type characteristics are more frequently found among women (20%) and are considered to be more stereotypically feminine than masculine. For this reason the NFs are the most unlike stereotypical males.

AN OVERVIEW OF THE DREAMERS

The characters in this chapter are Pablo, the organist at Ted's church, an ENFJ; Dean, the pastor at Ted's church, an INFJ; Jerry, the church youth group leader, an ENFP; and Eliot, a psychologist, an INFP. See table 11 in the appendix for a summary of each man's dominant and auxiliary functions and communication style. As in the previous chapters, the description of each of these characters will be followed by a prototype describing the more general characteristics of each type in the NF group.

Of the four types I have called the Dreamers, two of them, Pablo and Jerry, are extraverts; Pablo is an extraverted feeling type and Jerry is an extraverted intuitive type. The other two, Dean and Eliot, are introverts. Dean is an introverted intuitive type, and Eliot is called an introverted feeling type. We can see from this that while I call the NF group the Dreamers, there is actually one extraverted feeling type and one introverted feeling type, as well as an extraverted intuitive type and an introverted intuitive type. So the NF group consists of two feeling types and two intuitive types.

All of the NFs have some measure of heightened feeling and intuition, and as a consequence of that, some measure of undeveloped thinking and sensation as well. But the ways in which each of them uses their feeling is different. They all prefer to use feeling processes in combination with intuition. Their preference is to primarily use their intuition as a perceptual process and their feeling as an evaluative process. The overall mental process of the NF can be characterized thus:

> NF people typically possess the same personal warmth as SF people, since they use feeling for purposes of judgment. However, since they prefer intuition to sensing for purposes of perception, they do not center their attention upon concrete situations. Instead, they focus their interest upon possibilities, such as new projects, things that have never happened but might be made to happen, or truths that are not yet known but might be. NF types are typically interested in the complex-

ities of communication. Intuition provides an interest in patterns underlying immediate facts, symbolic meanings, and theoretical relationships. Feeling provides the interest in using these intuitive insights in human relationships.[1]

As we have seen in the last three type groups, each function of consciousness also has a particular orientation to time. Intuitive types' orientation to time is largely to the future. But for feeling types that relation to time is to the past.[2]

I call the NF group the Dreamers because, in one way or the other, all of them are preoccupied with feeling values and possibilities. Harmony among people, visions of possibilities, idealism, and compassion permeate the most important concerns and interests of NFs. These are their dreams, what has been and how it can be better. They are less concerned with the way people and the world are in the present, because to all NFs both could always be better. They tend to live in the possibilities of the future rather than the realities of the present. In wanting things to be better they are impatient but determined to make a difference.

Because their underdeveloped functions are sensation and thinking, NFs are less concrete, less practical, and less objective than most other men in the world. Because of their idealism and their enjoyment of relationships, Dreamers are frequently found in professions that promote comfort, care, and the resolution of conflict. Matters that are psychological, emotional, relational, and spiritual are like magnets for their interest.[3]

The extraverted NFs, such as Jerry and Pablo, are warm, sincere, and outgoing. Above much else, they enjoy easygoing, compatible contacts with others. True to the nucleus of their type, their interests often lie in what could be rather than what is. Often, they are the world's peacemakers and peacekeepers.

But they can also be revolutionaries when their ideals feel compromised by what they perceive as a cold and hostile world.

The introverted NFS, like Dean and Eliot, have feeling values as strong as the extraverts, but these reside beneath a misleading surface that may cause them to appear almost indifferent. Until one knows them well, they may appear cool or even aloof. But underneath that surface are strongly held compassionate human values. Compared to extraverted Dreamers, the introverts are usually more difficult to get to know and to understand.

The introvert's idealism is often less obvious than the extravert's because it is usually internalized and expressed by a need to have meaning and purpose in their lives and to help others find the same. They typically want to make a positive contribution to the world, but they are likely to make their contributions from behind the scenes—quietly, and in solitude.

Because of their overt desire to be of help, affirm, and bring out the best in others, NFS are the most frequently represented males in both clinical psychology and psychiatry. Often gifted writers, speakers, and persuaders, they can also be found in the "helping professions," in upper-level teaching, and sometimes in research. In spite of their rarity in the general population they are vastly overrepresented in both the helping professions as well as among writers.

COMMUNICATION STYLES OF THE NFS

The two FJS of this group, Pablo (ENFJ) and Dean (INFJ), communicate largely through feeling. The two TPS, Jerry (ENFP) and Eliot (INFP), communicate most often through intuition. All four of them use feeling in combination with intuition.

NFs discuss insights, concepts, and ideas, particularly as they pertain to other people, the human condition, and what is possible in the future. They like to discuss novel challenges and future opportunities. Their speech is highly imaginative, filled with hunches and speculation. Their style is more florid, and can be rambling, but is always interesting. They embellish their points with metaphors, analogies, and many-sided examples. They expect others' speech to be novel, unusual, and challenging. Their approach may be difficult to follow. It may seem disorganized and even disconnected, but they may return to their point, even after others have lost it. They have varied interests, enjoy conversation about most anything, and are capable of talking and listening almost endlessly.

RELATIONAL STYLES OF THE NFs

NFs are traditional in relationships but in a more idealizing than conservative way. They are empathic, warm, caring, and gentle with others. They often have high and unrealistic expectations of their partners. They daydream about most everything, and especially of meeting their soul mate when they have none. They like the idea of sharing everything, and are probably the most egalitarian of men in relationship. To NFs reality is an unnecessary and unwanted burden, even when they know better. They like to be of help by offering their understanding and options to others.

PABLO: AN EXTRAVERTED FEELING TYPE: ENFJ

Pablo, an ENFJ, has much in common with Phil (ESFJ), Teddy's teacher, who is also an extraverted feeling type. Pablo's auxiliary function is introverted intuition. Pablo is a public relations consultant. He is also the church organist at the same church Ted belongs to. Both Pablo and Ted are members of the church board. As a fellow board member, Ted has had many interactions with Pablo, leading to a friendship between them at church.

As a child, Pablo was outgoing and easy to get along with. He had many friends and was often at the center of activities during and after school. He was already tuned into the needs of others and careful to live up the expectations his parents had of him. Pablo developed verbal skills at an early age and by the time he was in high school he was a member of the debate team.

Pablo is a spontaneous, enthusiastic, and articulate leader in the church community. In particular, his natural warmth toward Ted has instilled a degree of confidence in their relationship that Ted is otherwise rarely open to. Ted admires Pablo's enthusiasm and apparent ease in getting along with almost everyone in the church. He also respects and admires his ability as an accomplished organist. Since being liked by others is so important to Pablo, Ted's respect and admiration create a special feeling of mutual camaraderie between them.

Pablo's naturalness and congenial style allow him to easily open conversations with Ted about his family life; he is particularly interested in Ted's son. Pablo appreciates Teddy's quiet, warm manner but also expressed his concern that in church activities, Teddy often seems withdrawn. Pablo's comments about Teddy on one occasion prompted Ted to remark that he wished Teddy were doing better in school. Pablo spontaneously reacted to this, inwardly relating Ted's concern to observations of him at meetings of the church council. While he understood that Ted could be efficient and practical in administrative matters, he saw that he was probably lacking in a feeling approach to his son.

Like other ENFJs, Pablo is quick to identify discord between others. He used his conversation with Ted as an opportunity to offer some advice and help for Teddy. Using his extraverted intuition, Pablo suggested a number of possible approaches Ted might take in trying to understand Teddy. He also suggested that Ted might want to talk to Dean, the minister of the church, about his problem with Teddy.

In terms of relational styles, Ted and Pablo are shadow types for each other. The potential shadow projection arises because the nucleus of each of their types (ST and NF) are in opposition. Further, since Ted's communication and relational style is primarily through extraverted thinking while Pablo's is primarily through extraverted feeling, their communication has the potential to easily go astray. But as we have seen here, there are some benefits that can come out of their interactions as well. This is particularly true when they are communicating about someone else, and not about each other.

In general, the judging aspect of type is best used in evaluating oneself, and ought to be reserved for that, and not used to judge others. On the other hand, the perceiving function is best used in one's perceptions about others. Since Pablo's auxiliary function is introverted intuition, he can use that in his perceptions of what Ted's difficulty with Teddy might be. Since Ted's intuition is close only to his least developed introverted feeling, it is not likely to be very developed. This creates a tendency to perceive mostly negative possibilities, especially when it comes to feeling issues.

THE ENFJ PROTOTYPE (3%)

Feeling → Intuition → Sensation → Thinking

There are not a lot of ENFJs in the entire population, and among men, they account for only 2.8 percent. (There are twice as many among women, about 4.5 percent.) Extraverted feeling (dominant) with introverted intuition (auxiliary) is a rare type for a man to be, and a difficult one unless he finds suitable channels for expressing his warmth, compassion, and attention to the needs of others.

While they share extraversion with the majority of men, ENFJs are not at all like most men because of the strength and dominance of their feeling side. They are probably the ultimate "harmonizers" and derive a great deal of satisfaction from being with others in warm, congenial contacts. In a society where most men value rationality, logic, and objectivity, some of the best ENFJ traits in males may be downplayed or even undervalued by other men, if not by the ENFJ himself.

The ENFJ man is one who values harmonious human contacts; he is a gregarious, congenial, sensitive, and empathic individual interested in promoting some aspect of human welfare. He is the "great friend," loyal and devoted as well as conscientious with those close to him. He has a great capacity to see many sides of an issue and other points of view. This ability can sometimes be frustrating to friends who appeal to them to take one side or the other, or a particular point of view.

> ENFJs tend to have curiosity for new ideas as such, taste for books and academic interests in general, tolerance for theory, vision, and insight, and imagination for new possibilities beyond what is present or obvious or known. ENFJs are likely to have a gift of expression, but they may use it in speaking to audiences rather than in writing.[4]

ENFJs want to find an agreeable way to be of service to others. For this reason they are often found in professions that provide human services, such as the clergy, social work, psychology, psychiatry, counseling, writing, acting, and consulting.

Since ENFJs are extraverted and judging, they like to have their dealings in the outer world organized and decided. At the same time they are not fanatics about organization. They are rarely interested in making a lot of money unless it also fulfills their need to be of service to others. Because of their popularity, they sometimes rise to positions of power and prestige. They are inclined to use their position and status for the good of the organization or a cause they believe in.

In relationships, the ENFJs are romantic, loyal, idealistic, and devoted to the needs of their partners. They truly enjoy relating and, being highly verbal and articulate, they like to talk with their partners about plans and goals for the future of their relationship. As much as possible they promote good will and harmony and avoid conflict and criticism. They like neither giving nor recieving negative feedback. They have strong affectional needs and can seem touchy or overly sensitive when these needs are ignored or neglected. They tend to idealize their partners and are often surprised and disappointed when their expectations go unrealized.

As fathers, ENFJs are enthusiastic, energetic, and accepting of their children. It is important for them to spend time with their children in activities that have meaning to them and that promote family togetherness. They want to promote a sense of well-being for everyone in the family. They are also often highly social and mix well with other families. They are likely to belong to several organizations that support their idealistic and humanitarian values.

They are enthusiastic supporters of their children; extraverted children enjoy their participative style. On the other hand, introverted children may find them overwhelming at times and may need to be left alone more than would please their convivial fathers. A father's sensitive feeling can be easily hurt by introverted childen simply because they sometimes need to be left alone. The extraverted feeling father needs to be able to see this withdrawal as a function of the child's natural introversion and not a reflection on him.

On the downside, ENFJs are quite sensitive to criticism, and because they have a tendency to idealize relationships they may not be open to confrontation. Sometimes they have a tendency to ignore the writing on the wall until it explodes in their faces. While they are often quite solicitous of the needs of others, they may not allow enough space and time for their own. Others may see them as not needing as much as they actually do. Since they so often hold such strong faith and trust in what they believe in, they may be disappointed more often than others when projects or relationships don't turn out as they expect them to. So it is difficult for them to acknowledge what they don't *want* to be true.

FREQUENT OCCUPATIONS OF ENFJs

Clergyman	Educational counselor
Religious worker	Therapist
Priest	Designer
Monk	Musician
Actor	Health teacher
Entertainer	Art teacher
Writer	Drama teacher
Artist	Music teacher
Consultant	English teacher
Vocational counselor	Psychologist

DEAN: AN INTROVERTED INTUITIVE TYPE: INFJ

Dean, an INFJ, is the other introverted type in our sample. Like Alexander (INTJ), he is quite a determined person, but since extraverted feeling rather than extraverted thinking is his auxiliary function, he is more interested in working with people than he is in the realm of ideas and intellectual pursuits. He is deeply respected by the members of his congregation. He is perhaps best admired for his eloquence in delivering sermons that are both inspirational and persuasive. The analogies he makes from biblical quotes to real-life concerns are imaginative and sometimes even provocative.

Because Dean's interest in working with people is so strong, he almost appears to be an extravert. His vision of the ideal church is one in which the members share a deep sense of community that extends beyond the confines of the immediate church. This idealism has sometimes been a bone of contention with the church board, who for the most part believe that their primary focus should be on matters closer to home.

Since he also has a degree in pastoral counseling, Dean was happy to discuss with Ted the difficulty with Teddy in depth. He listened compassionately and quietly to Ted as he described in detail what he felt the problem was. Dean's gentle manner and warm acceptance of Ted allowed him to feel safe in discussing the problem.

Following their talk Dean made two suggestions. One was that Teddy should become involved in the church youth group, where he would have more opportunities to interact with boys apart from family and school. He reminded Ted that Jerry, the youth group leader, had an unusual capacity to bring out and affirm the best in the members of the youth group. Dean felt that Jerry's emphasis on the importance of self-expression, as well as his ability to facilitate interaction between the boys in the group, would help to bring out the best in Teddy. Second, he suggested that Ted get a psychological consultant, to see if Teddy might need some supportive psychotherapy.

True to his extraverted thinking dominance, Ted was a little disappointed that Dean didn't have more of a reaction or more specific feedback about what was "wrong" with Teddy, but he did agree to follow the advice. Dean is an introvert, but like Pablo, his relational style is feeling (auxiliary extraverted feeling). Because of this he was not apt to judge what was "wrong" with Teddy or analyze the causes for his behavior. He was more concerned with the possible ways (primary introverted intuition) in which Teddy might be helped.

THE INFJ PROTOTYPE (2%)

Intuition → Feeling → Thinking → Sensation

Introverted intuition with extraverted feeling is the most rare type among men, occuring in only 1.6 percent of the population. (It is also the most rare among women, occurring in only 2 percent of the entire female group.) This rarity is further enhanced by the INFJs lack of visibility. Their introversion, need for privacy, dislike of groups, and avoidance of large organizations and bureaucracies keep them behind the scenes.

INFJs are often original thinkers who like conceptual abstractions. They have great respect for advanced education and are often successful students. For many INFJs, higher education is also a vehicle for their pursuit of innovative ideas in the field of human services.

INFJs are deeply committed, intense, and can be driven in pursuit of their inspirations. They are quiet, personable individualists whose influence and inspiration often emerge gradually only after years of solitude, concentration, and apparent stillness.

Often early in life INFJs have the idea that they have a gift to give and, more than that, they feel they must find the necessary means to develop their capacity to share it with others. As introverts, they pursue their futuristic and idealistic aims quietly, deeply, and diligently. A high regard for the well-being of others is often paramount in the application of their ideas and visions.

INFJs not only have a natural desire to understand themselves and human nature but also want to discover a comprehensive frame of reference in which to fit their ideas. For example, those who are physicians, psychiatrists, and psychologists are most likely to ascribe to wholistic paradigms of mental and physical health. They are the least reductive in trying to understand themselves and others, believing as they do in the importance of the interdependence of physical, emotional, and spiritual causes of human problems.

With friends and family, INFJs are insightful, sensitive, compassionate, and nurturing. As men, theirs is a difficult type to be because their scarcity, interests, and values make their form of masculinity atypical.

INFJ men are some of the most gentle and dedicated fathers, but they are not effusive in expressing their affection to their children. They express their love through thoughtful attention, interest, understanding, and by freely giving their time. They often do not have high performance expectations of their children. Instead they try to bring out their children's interests and special qualities, and to provide opportunities for their expression.

It is unfortunate that this type occurs so infrequently. Those INFJs who are able to bring their innovative visions to fruition often make significant contributions to the welfare of humankind.

On the downside, INFJs need to be on guard the possibility that they will fail to assert themselves in the face of opposition. INFJs sometimes fail to communicate their need for limits and boundaries with others. They fully expect others to regard what their idealism tells them is right, but when that doesn't happen they may be deeply hurt—and if that happens, they often keep their pain to themselves. And like the ENFJs, they may not express their own needs as much as they need to. They also tend to keep the natural depth of their insights to themselves for too long. And since their inferior function is extraverted sensation, they may also have trouble with the concrete details that are needed to manage their outer lives.

FREQUENT OCCUPATIONS OF INFJs

Priest	Psychiatrist
Monk	Social scientist
Clergyman	High school teacher
English teacher	University professor
Art teacher	Educational consultant
Drama teacher	Media specialist
Music teacher	Physician
Religious educator	Pathologist
Social worker	

JERRY: AN EXTRAVERTED INTUITIVE TYPE: ENFP

Jerry, an ENFP, was a Dreamer almost from the day he was born. As a child he seemed continually lost in reverie—when there were no other children to play with, his imagination was his best friend. He was interested in myriad projects, ideas, and fantasies, often more than his friends or parents could keep up with. Warning signs of his lack of organizational ability could also be seen in the way he failed to keep track of toys, pencils, and paper. Sensate reality seemed to be lost on him at an early age. One of his most obvious traits was his tendency to overpersonalize remarks, criticism, or even benign comments. He often seemed unusually emotional, sensitive, and vulnerable.

Today, Jerry is the leader of the church's youth group. He is a journalist as well as the editor of the church paper. Jerry, like Ted's nephew Paul, has extraverted intuition as his dominant function. But unlike Paul, whose auxiliary function is introverted thinking, Jerry's auxiliary function is introverted feeling. The combination of extraverted intuition and introverted feeling gives him what can be a seemingly endless enthusiasm for projects involving people. He is a favorite in church because of his enthusiastic, outgoing, and gregarious relational style. Like other ENFPs, Jerry is a pleaser, always eager to gain the acceptance and approval of others. Using his position as editor of the church paper, he has been influential in convincing many members of the church to support Dean's plan for community service.

But Jerry's style often makes Ted skeptical of him. While he appreciates Jerry's church work, many times he has seen that Jerry has difficulty following through on some of his ideas. He knows that Jerry usually requires a host of others to help implement the projects he initiates and is so enthusiastic about. Jerry is also likely to let the routine details of his personal life slip and frequently has a lot of catching up to do at home. For Ted, following through to completion is simply the natural conclusion of an idea.

Jerry strikes Ted as overly enthusiastic, almost unreal at times in his zeal to be positively affirming. And because Jerry's own need for affirmation is pretty obvious, this make Ted further suspect he might not be quite "real." Ted tends to think of Jerry as a "bull in the china shop."

Ted is uncertain about Teddy's participation in the church youth group with Jerry. He feels that Jerry, like Phil, may be too indulgent, too emotional, and generally too easy with Teddy. When he observes Jerry's ease in physically reaching out to Teddy, it makes him uncomfortable. Ted further believes that Jerry might tend to be unrealistic in his support of Teddy and not have firm enough expectations of him. On the other hand, although he would never say so, Jerry thinks of Ted as too stiff, formal, and rigid. He isn't surprised that Ted has so much trouble relating to his son.

Ted and Jerry's relational styles are quite opposed—one is often the shadow of the other. Ted's relational style is through thinking and Jerry's is through intuition. Each of their dominant functions is, at best, only the tertiary function of the other. And even though they are both extraverted, their extraversion has a very different quality and direction. Because these two have so little in common they are fertile carriers of each other's negative projections. The fact that Ted is a judging type and Jerry is a perceiving type influences their basic uncertainty about each other; Jerry is likely to feel controlled by Ted, and Ted is likely to see Jerry as too changeable and inconsistent.

THE ENFP PROTOTYPE (6%)

Intuition → Feeling → Thinking → Sensation

Men with extraverted intuition and introverted feeling comprise only 6 percent of men. (Among women, this type numbers about 9.5 percent.)

The ENFP is one of the most socially and occupationally versatile of men. Because of this versatility they are more difficult to describe as a group. They are the spontaneous, flexible innovators guided by inspirations often related to helping others. With friends they are warm, encouraging, and supportive. Their need to affirm others is matched by an equal need to be approved of themselves. They like to bring out the best in those they know and are frequently an inspiring influence. The human potential movement was something that could have been inspired by an ENFP.

Intellectually, ENFPs are original, curious, and imaginative. They enjoy academics and often have broad creative interests that span widely divergent subjects. They have an unusual capacity to see many sides of an issue and can explain complicated ideas simply and in several different novel ways. In some areas they may not go deep enough, preferring to command a sweeping view of many different subjects. They may have a streak of dilettantism.

As partners, ENFPs are nurturing, idealistic, and romantic, yet they have high expectations of their loved ones—even if those expectations aren't often spelled out. Women often like the ENFP man because of his sensitivity and his willingness to look at himself, as well as his willingness to work on improving his relationship. They enjoy many and varied activities with their partners and enjoy discussing all the places they would like to go—as long as they don't have to be the ones to actually make the travel plans. Having a partner who is a J is both a blessing and source of irritation to the ENFP because the judging partner often picks up their loose ends, but also reminds them when they are not doing their fair share of the "detail" work.

As fathers, they are affirming and supportive. They try to encourage their children to follow and cultivate their individual interests. They are not likely to be pushy or have unwarranted expectations. They want their children to have every opportunity to be everything they can be.

A great deal of the downside of ENFPs revolves around their difficulty in keeping up with all of the details in their personal and professional life. This is exacerbated by the fact that their zealousness causes them to bite off more than they can handle. They can be the worst procrastinators of all the types, feeling terribly burdened by the incidental things that always need to be done. Since they are so unstimulated by life's concrete realities, they prefer to ignore them or put them off, often with dire consequences. They frequently find themselves embarrassed by the fact that they haven't been able to deliver their promises, not because of insincerity, but because they often don't have the skills to take care of details. Men in high-level managerial positions may be particularly vulnerable this way because the administrative demands are so high. They need to learn to set aside the necessary time to take care of the mundane, or develop skill in mandating work to others. Their own visions may tend to fail because of their lack of follow-through.

Men who have inferior sensation may have to learn to go through an auxiliary function to accomplish what needs to be done. For example, the ENFP might appeal to his feeling function in order to master details. To do this he might appeal to the impact on his feeling that might result from imagining the possible ways he could approach taking care of details.

FREQUENT OCCUPATIONS OF ENFPs

Writer	Psychologist
Journalist	Speech pathologist
Rehabilitation counselor	Public relations worker
Art teacher	Clergyman
Drama teacher	Musician
Music teacher	Composer

ELIOT: AN INTROVERTED FEELING TYPE: INFP

As it turns out, the psychologist to whom Teddy was referred is Eliot, an INFP. Teddy and Eliot both have introverted feeling as their dominant function and extraverted thinking as their least developed function. As introverted feelers, they have a great deal in common, but also some differences that can make working together interesting and productive. Since Eliot understands introverted feelers well, he knew even before meeting Teddy that he would likely be slow to warm up. In the course of the interview he knew he would need special patience and encouragement to open up communication with Teddy beyond the superficial.

Since both Teddy and Eliot have inferior extraverted thinking, communicating on a thinking level or trying to solve problems in that way would be a difficult course to pursue. Teddy's father had already tried using logic and reason with him, and this extraverted thinking approach had left them both feeling frustrated and confused.

Since Teddy's auxiliary function is extraverted sensation, his relational style requires more than verbal expression. Using more concrete therapy materials such as clay, pencils, and paint would give him more specific access to expressing himself than he would have just talking. This would allow Teddy to use his natural communication style, extraverted sensation, to express himself.

As we have seen before, the auxiliary functions of introverts are also their relational styles, or the means by which they most relate to others. Since Teddy's relational style is sensation, he is drawn to the practical, more realistic aspects of outer life. But when there is overreliance on sensation, intuition is left unexplored and undeveloped. With no counterbalancing intuition to see new possibilities, Teddy can become stuck with a resigned attitude of "that's just the way things are." Teddy especially needs help with seeing other possibilities since extraverted intuition is his inferior function. Drawing on his own relational style of intuition, Eliot can help Teddy begin to think also in terms of how things *might* be, opening up for him positive possibilities that might lead to a better orientation to his future. He is also aware that all introverted feeling types (himself included) need to find ways to express their inner ideals. They need to develop confidence in themselves and greater awareness of their perfectionistic tendencies.

Eliot interviewed first Ted and his wife, then Teddy by himself, and then all of them together. Each of them was asked to complete the Myers-Briggs Type Indicator. Eliot also paid a visit to Teddy's classroom to observe him and to talk with his teacher, Phil. The assessment of Teddy's type included in the evaluation revealed that he was in need of a more personally relevant and practical approach to learning.

Eliot was able to explain to both Teddy's parents and Phil that for children of Teddy's type, the conventional, structured academic approach is a "turn-off" that only grows worse as they progress through school. In fact, this type frequently drops out of school because the academic situation is rarely relevant to their direct, practical, and experiential approach to learning. Eliot suggested that, in his own way, Teddy was already trying to incorporate this approach himself by drawing horses and daydreaming about what he could do outside of the classroom.

Eliot encouraged Phil's attention to Teddy but also reminded him that Teddy's introverted feeling is much more difficult to bring out than it might appear. He suggested that Phil incorporate some personally relevant approaches to learning for him and give him support and encouragement for succeeding in those ways. For example, Teddy might be encouraged to share some of what he was learning about horses with the class, or write papers and do drawings about it. Calling on Teddy more often and encouraging him to verbalize what he was thinking might help him feel less withdrawn and break into his cycle of daydreaming.

At the parents' meeting, Eliot also discussed with Ted the difference between his type and Teddy's. He pointed out that Ted's appreciation of more structured learning situations worked very well for him when he was in school. However, Teddy was not stimulated by that approach and would never be as successful at it as his father had been. Teddy was actually learning a tremendous amount from his more practical experience. Ted agreed with that, and admitted that he hadn't thought of it in that way before.

Eliot also pointed out that, contrary to Ted's impression, his approval was very important to Teddy. Teddy probably just didn't know how to go about getting it. Without his father's approval, Teddy was beginning to withdraw because he felt incapable of ever measuring up. He was also beginning to devalue his own way of being since it wasn't like his father's. If this continued it would eventually reduce his sense of self-esteem and self-worth, and he would be even less willing to put effort into his work. Eliot remarked that Teddy also needed to know that he had qualities that his father liked and approved of. He suggested that Ted might think about some qualities of Teddy's he admired, especially ones different from his own, and occasionally mention these to him in a positive way.

Observing Ted, Eliot could tell that he put himself under a lot of pressure at work and wondered if Teddy might be indirectly feeling some of that from him. This allowed Ted to open up more about his own frustration, his struggles at work, and the fact that his physician had suggested that his blood pressure and stomach troubles might be reflections of stress. Eliot recommended that Ted try a stress-reduction class as well as biofeedback training to learn more positive control of his symptoms. Stress management made sense to Ted since he was aware that major businesses were beginning to incorporate this type of program to reduce manager job stress. After Eliot explained the nature of biofeedback, Ted thought he might be willing to try it since it was practical, logical, and followed a definite predictable treatment plan. Eliot also knew that biofeedback, as a "scientific" approach, was often the door through which extraverted thinking types could be introduced to the very real relationship between their emotions and their body symptoms.

THE INFP PROTOTYPE (3%)

Feeling → Intuition → Sensation → Thinking

Introverted feeling with an auxiliary function of extraverted intuition is probably the most difficult type for a man to be. The INFP shares neither the extraversion (75 percent) nor the thinking dominance (65 to 70 percent) of the male group. Further, he does not share the sensation preference with 70 percent of the total population. Because the INFP's dominant function represents the inferior function (introverted feeling) of a major part of the population, someone who has that type as a dominant function is a potential shadow carrier for most other men. Considering the fact that extraverted feeling women (25 percent of the female population) and extraverted feeling males (11 percent of the male population) are in such direct opposition to INFPs, a good 75 percent of the population may think of them as being "a little strange." INFPs, in turn, may think of three-quarters of the population as having little in common with them.

The INFP is a quiet, gentle, good-humored, introspective man who *must* find meaning in his life. The INFP is a principled idealist whose values may not be obvious to others until they are challenged or disregarded. Only then does the tenacity with which he holds these values become apparent. Others are then taken aback by the INFP's unexpected departure from his usual *laissez-faire* attitude.

He is a determined achiever who goes about his quest in a reserved, almost inconspicuous way. His need for meaning pervades all aspects of his life—work, relationship, and ultimately, life itself. So important is meaning to the INFP man that without it he feels lost, depressed, and forlorn, as though he has been deserted by life. Even in childhood INFPs may dream about making a meaningful contribution to humanity. Often the childhood fantasy of later life includes becoming famous or at least well known for their contribution. However, being introverted, they rarely reveal this fantasy to others. The fantasy of fame may arise as a compensation for the seemingly paradoxical way in which his introversion is combined with a great need to make a contribution to the world.

INFPs must find occupations that provide opportunities to express their deeply held values. They are perhaps the least likely to be driven by conventional masculine standards of external success. Their fathers, particularly if they are STs, need to understand this about them. To insist that the INFP son find success in conventional task-oriented jobs is to miss the critical importance of his search for meaning. Further, the INFP son deprived of his own values by his father's expectations is likely to become a rebel. More often than not, his life work must provide a feeling that he is offering a valuable, needed service to those around him. And because of his perfectionism, this work needs to be done well.

In relationship, the INFP is committed, faithful, dedicated, and eager to please. The INFP household is often aesthetically pleasing and marked by comfort, security, and symbolic reminders of important values and experiences. For INFPs the home is certainly the castle.

As all else in life for INFPs, relationships are potentially filled with meaning. This may extend to the idea of working with a loved one toward a mutually humanitarian goal or contribution. Perhaps more than for any other of the men, the INFP sees a soul mate as necessary to the full realization of relationship. Relationship for him cannot be only conventionally successful and functional, it must embody the feeling that his partner shares his idealistic values. Love relationships are sometimes difficult for INFPs because they tend to project their grandiose idealism onto potential partners and are often disappointed to find their loved ones don't match their ideals.

INFP parents are often liberal, tolerant, and supportive of what they perceive as their children's special abilities. Only rarely do they impose unfeasible expectations on their children. They want their children to realize their potential and feel good about themselves. At times, they may be so accepting that to their children they seem unconcerned. This is particulary so for ST, NT, and SF children, who often seek specific directions and expectations from their parents.

Even though INFP fathers are particularly sensitive to bringing out and encouraging their children's unique talents, their children are also apt to carry their father's idealistic projections. For this reason, what the father has failed to accomplish often surfaces as subtle expectations of his child. The INFP's sons are especially fertile carriers of their father's unfulfilled potentials. Daughters may also be expected to embrace their father's ideals even when they choose different paths.

On the downside, INFPs may become myopic, not able to see beyond their own dreams to the needs of others. Because extraverted thinking is their inferior function, they also may not be objective or impersonal enough in their analysis of what it is they have to say. They can become so preoccupied with their own visions and expectations of themselves that they fail to take into sufficient account the demands of their outer lives and others around them. Their inner vision can be so strong that they even neglect the proper care of their bodies and health.

The INFPs also need to ground their ideals by finding practical applications for them. As perfectionists, it is often difficult for them to find all of the opportunities that meet their needs. And without specific opportunities to realize their life goals, they become disillusioned, disheartened, and depressed. INFPs who fail to find their niche in life may live out an aspect *puer aeternus* archetype—the eternal boy—forever in search of something beyond what he has, what he has accomplished, or who he is.

FREQUENT OCCUPATIONS OF INFPs

Psychiatrist	Composer
Psychologist	Reporter
Writer	Journalist
Artist	Religious educator
Editor	Social scientist
Social worker	Education consultant
Teacher	Counselor
Musician	Rehabilitation counselor

SUMMARY OF THE NF GROUP

The intuitive feeling types comprise only 14 percent of the entire male population. Since their perceiving mode is intuition, NFs look for the possibilities or patterns of things, rather than just for the facts themselves. Like the sFs, this group is interpersonally warm and typically interested in work that involves direct contact with people. Their use of the feeling function puts their intuitive perceptions in the service of human relationships, rather than at the service of more impersonal analysis, as in the case of the NTs.

Perhaps the most cardinal characteristic of the NF group is the need to discover a sense of personal meaning in life. For this reason, they are the men most interested in psychotherapy, men's groups, personal growth, and the human potential movement. They are more impressed by the symbolic than the literal. Mythology, folklore, fairy tales, and poetry are all natural interests for them. NFs are the communicators and the questers, forever seeking the value that lies beyond the actual. They are the singers of the "Impossible Dream."

The championing of humanistic causes is frequently also a passionate vocation or preoccupation for them. In the extreme, the NF is the guru, soulmaker, or visionary. His pursuit is first, last, and always the pursuit of meaning, significance, and self-realization. NFs who fail to find an outer cause in life or who are not successful in finding some semblance of personal meaning often end life as bitter, resentful, and unfulfilled men. All NFs are convinced that in some way, the world ultimately makes sense and life *should* have meaning. It is their quest to find what that meaning is; to not find it means to suffer unbearable depression and disillusionment.

NF men are also the most unconventionally masculine of the four major nuclear types. Their style often appears to have little in common with that of the sTs, who define the current concept of masculine. The sTs view and evaluate the world largely in concrete, practical, logical, and factual terms. Their superior functions, thinking and sensation, are the least developed in NF men. On the other hand, NFs view and evaluate the world not in terms of the way it actually is, but in terms of its possibilities for peace, harmony, and cooperation. The most developed functions of the NF men, feeling and intuition, are the least developed in ST men.

As we have seen, communication is most limited when the communicators differ on *both* the primary and secondary functions. Since this is exactly the case with STs and NFs, the ways in which they can communicate effectively are often quite limited. To communicate more effectively with STs, NFs need to try to be more objective, factual, and concise. And for STs to communicate more effectively with NFs, they need to try to be more personable, pay more attention to the process of communication rather than just the content, and acknowledge and emphasize areas of agreement as well as differences.

Since the ST males are the most typically masculine, NFs are especially likely to carry the shadow for them. Since NFs are also more likely to have ST fathers, their type may not be valued by their fathers, and NF males often grow up with a sense that their fathers, and generally other men as well, disapprove of them in some fundamental way—particularly in their search for meaning. ST males generally see NFs as too "wimpy," "touchy-feely," and even too "feminine." On the other hand, NF men, very much like many women, see ST men as "too linear," "overcontrolling," and "dominated by their intellects."

Another basic value difference between the STs and NFs lies in their divergent orientation to success. The STs seek satisfaction in objective, practical accomplishments. The NFs value fulfilling potentials and finding harmony between people. Perhaps the STs' greatest negative projecton onto the NFs is that "if the world was left to them, nothing would ever be accomplished." The NFS' greatest projection onto STS is that "the world *has* been left to them and look what they've done to destroy it."

The NTS, as the next most masculine group, are only a bit more tolerant of NFS. The SF group, the largest among women, is probably relationally closer to the NFS than either STS or NTS. For this reason NF males get along better with both SF men and women than with either the STS or NTS. However, they are much closer to women in temperament and often feel greater comfort in relating to women than they do with men. Of course, the NF men usually get along the best with NF men and women than any other group. Again, since they are much closer to women in temperament, they often feel greater comfort in relating to women than they do with men. Both NF males and SF females value harmony in relationship and interpersonal nurturance, and they are more interested in human rights.

For NFS, human relationships often become the fertile and primary ground for the application of relational possibilities in both personal and professional life. The downside of this is, because they give so much, they may not be seen as emotionally vulnerable and needy as they are. NFS often give the impression of "being on top of it all." This can be misleading because their sensitivity, vulnerability, and need for approval may not seem obvious to others. Because NFS have such a strong desire to be accepting and affirming of others, their difficulties may often revolve around being unwilling or afraid to set realistic limits for themselves and others. At times they may be too understanding and accepting of others with the result that they may be taken advantage of. Untempered idealism may sometimes cause them to set too lofty goals for themselves, leading to disappointment, frustration, and disillusionment. They may be poor judges of time, with the result that they fritter away precious moments being sidetracked by inefficient pursuits.

The practical, everyday demands of life for NFs may leave them with piles of unfinished projects, unpaid bills, and unkept commitments. The lack of attention to future planning for themselves, especially financially, may in the long run leave them facing retirement and old age with little left for themselves.

Their frequent lack of developed thinking may result in a form of unclear or unsubstantiated premises for their beliefs and ideas. They often feel that they don't really need proof for their ideas and are offended when others are not convinced or accepting of their point of view. At the other extreme, to prove their position, they may garner so many facts that they lose their audience in a mass of unnecessary or irrelevant details. They may have a tendency to become cavalier about the values of others or high-handed about their own.

As we have seen, in relationships the NF is likely to have idealizations of his partner that border on the archetypal. If his partner feels compelled to reach his lofty expectations of an idealized state of mutual bliss and understanding, there may be some deep troubles in store for them.

Within all of the members of the group, there is a strong literary and communicative aptitude. The extraverts, Jerry (ENFP) and Pablo (ENFJ), and the introverted intuitives with feeling communication styles, such as Dean (INFJ), often choose to express themselves through speech and teaching. The introverted feeling types with intuitive communication styles, such as Eliot (INFP), more often choose writing as the primary medium of communication.

Above all else, NFs value harmony in human relationships on both the personal and collective level. They often feel disillusioned that others don't see this need for peacefulness in the world.

Having finished with the NFs, we have discussed all of the sixteen psychological types of men. Hopefully, we now have a greater appreciation for the contribution of psychological type to both the similarities as well as the differences in the personalities of men. At the same time, other contributions to the psychological makeup of individual men allow for even greater diversity in their behavioral, emotional, and occupational potentialities.

So far, this largely structural framework has provided a relatively objective means for observing different types of men without, at the same time, rigidly categorizing them. Now we turn our attention to the more dynamic aspect of typology by looking at typology as a psychology of consciousness.

CHAPTER 7

Using Typology as a Psychology of Consciousness

Le cœur a ses raisons que la raison ne connaît point. (The heart has its reasons that reason knows nothing about.)
— Pascal

TYPOLOGY AS AN EVOLUTIONARY OUTCOME

Theoretically, our psychological type is a disposition we have been given at birth, however enhanced or modified it becomes through early learning experience. However, the fundamental split along gender lines between thinking and feeling that typology pinpoints may well describe a bigger picture: our current level of both "masculine" and "feminine" consciousness. Our psychological functions may have evolved along these lines to meet the biological and psychological demands placed on men and women throughout our entire evolutionary and social history.

If it is true that this typological split has been an evolutionary process, then in some ways men and women have both been served well by it. Women have been the primary carriers of feeling; men, of thinking. The refinement of feeling in women has served them in their roles as the primary caregivers of children, of providing nurturance and support to their partners, and for modeling society's affiliative values and needs. The evolution of the thinking function in men has served their need to objectively reason, make decisions, and impersonally run the outer world. But now it may be that in serving these needs, both masculine and feminine consciousness have become too one-sided and overly relegated to sex roles. They may indeed no longer serve the best interests of men and women.

AN ARCHETYPAL PATTERN OF THE MASCULINE

When masculine consciousness is extreme it incorporates particular aspects of the father archetype. This constellation characterizes men principally oriented to the outer world. Of most importance to them is what they produce and accomplish outside of themselves. They are practical, task-oriented, and their mental processes are dominated by impersonal logic and objective thinking.

The father archetype has both a positive and negative pole. The positive pole relates to productivity, law, order, stability, providing for and protecting the family, respect for established institutions, and, in many ways, a conventional approach to family life.

The negative pole, represented by the *senex* (old man), is dogmatic, rigid, overly conventional, and disconnected from the conscious use of positive feeling judgments. The negative father is emotionally cold and overcontrolling. He demands allegiance to his way, allows no room for opposing points of view or values, and in the extreme can be tyrannical or dictatorial. The negative father can reflect a "devouring" quality; he overcomes and subjugates others' feelings, wishes, and ambitions to his own. In the negative father's domain there is little room for the growth, individuality, or dissent of others; he demands allegiance and a repetition of his values.

A mythological image that reflects this masculine disposition is the Sky Father. The split from the Earth Mother or the archetype of the feminine is nowhere so apparent as in this one-sided portrayal of masculinity, because this constellation is so dissociated from the inner creativity and relational values of the feminine, endogenic principle. Here the masculine and feminine principles seem irreconcilably split.

The Sky Father embodies

> those attributes needed to fulfill the protector and provider roles. He is assertive, aggressive, competitive, and warlike. His interest is in techniques, facts, logic, and decision making. He is clear, precise, and focused. He worships light and power. He denies the importance of emotion, feeling, intuition, and the irrational. He leaves the unmeasurable, the uncanny, the fecund, the intimate, and the relational to his earth mother opposite.[1]

These attributes are analogous to those that characterized the rise of the patriarchy and the flourishing of the masculine, exogenic, or outer-world principle. Our fathers have given greater overt and covert sanction to the thinking function, but they have modeled little of the differentiated feeling function, and thus the feeling function is generally undeveloped in men.

In this chapter, we are going to look at how the feeling function manifests in men, and what they can do to raise it to consciousness, whether it is their actual inferior function and/or simply undeveloped or projected.

THE IMPORTANCE OF FEELING FOR MEN

As we saw earlier, the feeling function is an evaluative function that facilitates judgments about personal, feeling-related values. The feeling function weighs, evaluates, considers, and appraises. Its "object" may be emotions, people, or even ideas. A man can feel about what he thinks just as he can think about what he feels, but he can't use the thinking and feeling functions simultaneously. For feeling to be differentiated and maximally effective, a man must have the ability to access and use the function independently from other functions, but not rely on it exclusively. Overreliance on thinking may obstruct the easy flow of emotion. Developed feeling allows for control and reflection in our emotional life. But having feelings, emotions, or affects is not the same as using the feeling function. Closely aligned to the feeling function is the realm of emotional experience, which for most men is less close to the surface of consciousness than the thinking function, with its values that rely on logic and rationality for their truth.

The lack of development of the feeling function may result in a number of problems when feeling is overly global, of a poor quality, extremely introverted, or inferior. All of these problems may decrease the quality of emotional life, most notably the impact of poor feeling on emotional expression and relationships.

Global feeling judgments, such as "I love my country and will fight to the end to defend it," are simplistic, unreflective, and inappropriate. The statement does not include any discriminating judgment about context, the nuances of situation, condition, or mitigating circumstances. All of these must be considered so that feeling judgments won't be simple-minded. And since we often must be able to discriminate between differing values and even conflicting values, reflective processes are needed to make judgments clear and their application effective. Differentiated feeling requires time, patience, and a weighing of contexts.[2] The degree of conscious reflectiveness employed will decide the general quality of our feeling judgments.

Having little accessibility to consciousness, blocked emotion stagnates and erupts rather than flowing smoothly when it is needed and warranted. So, while the feeling function is not the same as emotion, it might be thought of as a door to emotional experience.

Especially for extreme thinking types, this door is not only often closed, but is also liable to open when least expected. If a thinking type is provoked in the wrong way, it sometimes just blows open. Eruptions of emotion in the thinking type are like strong gusts of wind that suddenly and unexpectedly come streaming in, apparently from "nowhere." The thinking type and those around him are often puzzled by both the intensity and the source of those eruptions.

As we have seen, feeling in the thinking types is often the least developed function. And when it is expressed, inferior feeling has a primitive quality because it has not been consciously attended to. As Marie-Louise von Franz points out:

> In a politician, the inferior feeling function might unconsciously manifest itself in a deep rooted and steadfast loyalty to his country. But it might also induce him to drop an atomic bomb or commit some other destructive act. Unconscious and undeveloped feeling is barbaric and absolute, and therefore sometimes hidden destructive fanaticism suddenly bursts out of the extraverted thinking type.[3]

Such an outburst seems to come from an outside, unknown source, provoked only by a wrongly timed criticism, or sometimes even by a rightly timed empathy. Then the thinker wonders, "Where did *that* come from?" When that happens, he didn't have the feeling, the feeling had him. Since it doesn't seem internal, it doesn't seem to really belong to the man who experiences it, who may then blame others for his emotion.

There also may be a childlike or naive quality to the feeling of the thinker, since it is so close to the unconscious, and at times totally immersed in it. He may be plagued by unpredictable moods, as well as irritations and annoyances with others that he does not understand. He also may be inexplicably mistrustful, jealous, and, in spite of himself, may lapse into irrelevant gossip. Or he may find something extremely funny without understanding why. These unbidden eruptions are out of character for the persona of the thinker, and he rarely bothers to see where they are coming from or what they mean.

This poor quality of feeling is a result of men learning early to blunt, dull, inhibit, and judge their feelings, and then spending much of their lives repeating these habits. In childhood the filtering of feeling may have served some purpose, it might have been necessary in order to survive emotionally. But the cost of so doing may leave us with only a one-dimensional sense of being, that is, emotionally barren, empty, lifeless, or stale. We end up doing what needs to be done, becoming efficient at taking care of what needs to be attended to, but knowing little of our feeling judgments about any of it. And we learn unfelt, monosyllabic answers like "fine," "good," "well" to questions about how we are feeling that say nothing about emotional richness, breadth, or depth.

There can be little transformation of one's psyche without owning and transforming one's feelings. Intellectual understanding increases one's fund of information, creates contexts, reasons, and rationalizations, but without deeply differentiated emotional awareness, there is rarely a real change in consciousness. The obsessive-compulsive becomes intellectually obsessed with his compulsions, but can't behave noncompulsively. A genuine change in consciousness means that one *grew* from the experience, not just that one had it, or even that one understood it. So feeling cannot be differentiated or transformed unless it is felt—as deeply as possible. It sounds simple to do, but isn't.

So, as a judging function, feeling works best when a man can learn to make *differentiated* judgments about his values, especially those regarding relationships.

WHEN FEELING IS INFERIOR

As we have seen, 22.4 percent of American males are extraverted thinkers, like Ted and Sheldon, who have inferior *introverted* feeling. (Introverted feeling, even when dominant, is virtually "invisible.") Another 11 percent are introverted thinkers, like Cal and Harry, who have inferior *extraverted* feeling. This means that feeling is the least accessible, least developed function for over one-third of men. For another third of men like Jake (ESTP), Richard (ISTJ), Paul (ENTP), and Alexander (INTJ), feeling is the tertiary function. In all, more than 60 percent of men have feeling that is either inferior or at best only their third preference. This is why we say that the majority of men have feeling as their most undeveloped function. And as we saw earlier, this undeveloped feeling has a dramatic effect on men's communication styles as well as their relationships.

A man's persona is the part of himself he chooses to present to the outer world. It is the part of himself most strongly defined by the role he plays in the outer world. The persona plays a role here as it often further hides his inferior function, especially if he feels he needs to behave in a very controlled, "masculine" way. If his persona finally falters in a stressful situation and his inferior feeling rises to the surface, it may explode in an embarrassing or humiliating way, as we have already discussed.

On the social and cultural level, men generally have developed high levels of competency in managing their outer lives through the use of their extraverted thinking. But much of their inner lives remain relatively impoverished. This is because they have neglected to consciously address, at least with any depth, the importance of emotional relatedness through conscious differentiation of their feeling function. Of course, stereotypes of masculinity often condition men not to express their inner life of feeling. Men's feeling function—even if it is dominant or auxiliary rather than inferior or tertiary—is influenced and conditioned by social expectations, sex roles, and their relationships with their fathers, mothers, and women generally. All of this has created a societal tendency to think that many men simply have "no feelings."

Of course there are no men without feelings, there are just those who appear to be, and for whom feeling is largely unconscious. What men seem to need now is to develop a more conscious appreciation of their own feeling function. The values we can develop by using this function consciously and deliberately may change the quality and meaning of our relationships and our values in the world. Feeling, as it is often mistakenly thought of, does not reside only in the domain of the feminine.

However, it is often only through mothers and women that many men have been able to identify and vicariously experience the feeling function. But in our need to disidentify with mothers and women, we have then also disidentified with feeling. In splitting from feeling we become overidentified with thinking. What remains is inferior feeling, connected with imagery of the wounded anima or the mother complex that is carried for us by women. When men unconsciously allow their mothers and outer women to carry feeling for them, they disown an essential psychological function needed for their full growth and wholeness. And as long as it remains undeveloped, it will be part of the personal and collective shadow of men, and it will continue to be carried by women.

On the other hand, women have become more active in moving beyond the socially sanctioned feeling roles they have played out in relationships with men. This is particularly true of their role as men's unconscious mothers. If men fail to develop their own feeling function, as well as lose these emotional support structures they have come to depend on, they will become increasingly depressed by the reemergence of their unmet dependency needs. Women's liberation, for example, has been experienced by many men as a symbolic reabandonment by the mother and the feminine. And this is happening at a time when they are ill-equipped to deal with the emotionally undeveloped parts of themselves.

ANIMA, MARRIAGE, AND TYPE

As men try to grow psychologically and emotionally, a signal task is to integrate parts of themselves that have never been developed, and particularly those lost through projection onto others. As we have seen, one means of projection involves the shadow. Another way involves the split from the inner feminine, which Jung called the *anima*. Jung described the anima as a man's contrasexual side, or the feminine representation of his unconscious. The images of his inner feminine are often found in his dreams, fantasies, and projections onto outer women. When men are dissociated from the anima, they may unconsciously try to connect with that missing part of themselves through relationships with women.

When a man projects the anima, an outer woman becomes the carrier of some of the most important undeveloped parts of himself. As a result, the man may suffer the loss of psychological and emotional energy. That missing energy is temporarily displaced onto an outer woman, who by embodying it becomes an object of desire, fascination, and promise.

An example of such projection is what happened to Cal (INTP) when he fell madly in love with Marci, one of his students. Marci was young, bright, beautiful, and vivacious. She seemed to cast a spell over Cal; he became fascinated with virtually every move she made. He loved the way she walked, talked, and even smiled. He found himself distracted by her presence in class, especially when he found her pale green eyes staring at him. Her body became a beguiling mystery, fraught with the promise of an excitement he thought he had never known. Her vitality made him feel alive in a way he barely remembered.

One day, she approached him on campus. As they stood together talking, he felt tipsy with the intoxication of her soft fragrance. When she touched his arm his legs felt molten. Being next to her seemed to reopen his senses and awaken feelings that had been dormant for years. Because of how she made him feel, he knew he had to have her.

But not long after he did, his passion cooled, the precious enchantment seemed to seep out of him. He was left feeling deflated, confused, depressed, and strangely empty. And the demons that had plagued him before he met her, the ones she seemed to make disappear, returned again whenever he tried to sleep.

As an extraverted feeling type, ESFJ, Marci was an especially apt carrier for his inner feminine. She was virtually the opposite of his type, INTP. She was able to carry his anima perfectly. As an ideal feminine representation of his unconscious, she was able not only to attract him but, even if temporarily, to captivate his soul. She personified the missing parts of his inner life.

Marci's youthfulness, energy, enthusiasm, and sexuality literally enlivened and replaced the staleness that had slowly ebbed in Cal's one-sided, middle-aged life. His own youth was spent almost entirely on getting an education and developing his career. After becoming a tenured professor, he spent even more time in academic and intellectual pursuits, causing the little emotional life he did have to dry up. He had become depressed and never fully understood why, nor did he bother to look into it. Had he developed more fully, by incorporating more of the feeling and sensation that Marci lived so intensely, he probably would not have felt possessed by her.

The carrier of a man's anima does not have to be his opposite type. Cal's case was extreme and it was certainly Marci's contrasting type that fueled the attraction. If Cal had actually married Marci, there undoubtedly would have been problems. In reality, only 4 percent of all married couples have all four functions opposite. And interestingly enough, the men most likely to marry complete opposites are the introverts with thinking.[4]

It is statistically most impractical for men and women to marry the same types. This is so simply because of the distribution of the types among the sexes, and particularly because there are so many more thinking men than thinking women, and so many more feeling women than feeling men. Therefore, most thinking type men are married to feeling type women. This configuration in marriage probably also lends unwarranted support to the idea that communication and relational styles are sex-based, rather than type-based.

This thinking-feeling polarity in couples presents men another opportunity for confrontations with their inferior function. This is borne out by the fact that many couples seeking therapy are often either typologically more different than similar to each other, or opposite-typed. But the available research on marriage and type indicate that most marriages occur between couples who have some elements in common and some different.

The statistical likelihood is that couples will have two preferences in common, but in actuality, most couples have three. The reason that opposite-typed couples seek treatment may be because that configuration produces more marital problems than it does in mixed type or same-type couples.

In my own experience, couples' most common problems are generated out of the male-thinking/female-feeling polarity. Even though there are fewer of them, couples with male-*feeling*/female-*thinking* combinations also seek out therapy for similar reasons. It is the opposites of the types that account for the problems, rather than which sex has which type.

In either case, the projections within the couple create a confrontation between each of their shadows. In the form of their partner, each finds the undeveloped parts of him- or herself staring them in the face. These shadow elements are always unexpected and are likely to be blamed on the ways in which one's partner "changed" in the course of the relationship. In truth, the shadow elements were always there, they just went unrecognized because the initial positive projections, "overshadowed the shadow."

In any case, the therapeutic value of oppositeness consists of the possibility that it may cause both partners to eventually come to terms with the most undeveloped parts of themselves. There can be a recognition on both sides that instead of blaming each other for being wrong, they can each gain mutual respect from recognizing that their partner is simply typologically different. If this is successful, the confrontation will result in the man becoming more conscious of his neglected feeling function and, in turn, the woman coming to terms with her undeveloped thinking function. That is the best-case scenario, where both gain rather than one or both losing. But this is easier said than accomplished.

For example, men who have introverted or extraverted thinking as their dominant function (one-third of all men) may initially value partners who possess an opposite attitude feeling function. As in Cal's problem with Marci, after a while this partner is likely to bring up their own most undeveloped function—inferior extraverted feeling or inferior introverted feeling. If his neglect of the feeling function has been extreme, as it often is in men who overemphasize objective, intellectualized aspects of life, the anima function is going to be infantile and in some cases even primitive.

So, the anima for a man with inferior feeling is often the opposite of his attitude type; extraverted men often marry the introverted anima, and introverted men, the extraverted anima. The opposite type attitude of his partner seems to provide an unconscious complementarity to the man's more conscious and dominant function. A potential problem, on the other hand, is that his undeveloped feeling function and the anima may exist in a contaminated state. That is to say, the outer woman he relates to and his inner feminine are confused, resulting in an inability to differentiate between what he is aware of feeling consciously and feelings that arise autonomously from his unconscious. This is particularly true when he is under stress, such as in an argument with his partner; at these times he may either be unable to articulate how he feels, or he may experience what I call an "anima attack," in which rather than "having" feelings, he is caught in the grip of primitive feelings which "have" him.

THE INFERIOR FUNCTION AND THE SHADOW

The inferior function and the shadow are intimately related since both share a place in the unconscious. Since the inferior function most often remains out of consciousness, it develops a peculiar autonomy and a mercurial ability to "liven things up" when we least expect it—and, often when we least want it. It is personified by the shadow character who shows up in our dreams, our fantasies, and in self-righteous projections placed on others as we attempt to relieve ourselves of our own worst traits.

When men have inferior feeling, their shadow (which is usually a male in men's dreams) may be contaminated or fused with the anima. A man who features himself to be very tough may see in his dreams an effeminate, sometimes overtly homosexual shadow, much to the chagrin of the dreamer. He may quickly forget the dream or perhaps interpret it only externally in terms of how bothered he is by homosexuality.

In a similar way, fathers sometimes unconsciously use their sons to carry projections of qualities they fear in themselves. Some bring their sons to therapy because they are concerned that they are becoming too much the sissy, or worry that they "may grow up to be homosexual." We can be somewhat sure that the problem lies in the father's shadow, and that his capacity to contain his inferior function is weakening. This usually spells trouble for the father more than for his son; once the father receives treatment, the son's "problem" usually goes away.

Another manifestation of a man's inability to contain the

shadow may take the form of sexual preoccupations, voyeurism, perversions, or a regression to the incest wish. Perhaps one of the worst forms of this, currently very much in the news, is the abduction of girls, or even boys, by men who have completely lost control of their shadow and inferior function. They act out the shadow problem without any restraint at all. It is as if they feel compelled to "possess" the anima in the most concrete possible way and to literally "take" her for themselves. This is the effect of a tremendous amount of previous repression finally breaking out in a man who often was seen before as someone who "wouldn't hurt a fly." Outbreaks of violence in previously passive men are a similar phenomenon. Outbreaks like these speak to the tremendous pressure built up by repression. This damming up of psychic energy creates a need for the inferior function to be released from its prison and into consciousness. Loss of control is often an indication that this internal pressure has grown too strong and is demanding some form of release.

In this respect, loss of control may have a positive component if it can be gradual rather than violent. It is the psyche's means of bringing disowned problems to awareness, since they haven't come to consciousness in a less damaging way. Even consistent failures can be viewed as an attempt, still unconscious, to establish a balance in the personality where there has been no conscious path to the real problem.

While working on the inferior function often seems bleak and even threatening, it can also be a surprising source of life and vitality. Our experience becomes fresh and new when we can make a conscious connection with a part of ourselves that has lain dormant too long. Since the inferior function is so intimately related to the unconscious, the creative potential of the unconscious also may be mobilized, providing new insights and approaches to problem solving.

TRYING TO RAISE THE INFERIOR FUNCTION

In the late sixties and early seventies, the arrival of encounter groups, sensitivity training, est, "rage reduction therapy," and so on, allowed many men previously outside of mainstream psychotherapy a number of collective opportunities to try out "getting in touch with themselves." Some therapists and group leaders encouraged men who had been disconnected from their feeling function all of their lives to "get it all out." Various techniques seemed to spring up almost overnight that were designed to liberate uptight men from their "cerebral hang-ups."

Many of the men who went through that got little more than trendy new vocabularies that told them how to talk about their feelings. First as a participant and later as a graduate student in psychology, I saw that few of the men I knew (myself included) were able to make changes of any depth in their feeling values. Some of us became more like caricatures of "feeling" men than individuals who developed any lasting depth. In some ways, that seemed worse than the way we were before. Some came away with a new vocabulary and a stilted style of relating, feeling wonderful and full of energy, but it was a state that only lasted a brief time.

More recently with the poet Robert Bly's "mythopoetic" emphasis gaining popularity in some contingents of the men's movement, men are being encouraged to get in touch with their "deep masculinity." This exhortation seems to be largely based on the erroneous notion that men have already integrated their feminine sides. Men are urged to "learn to shout" and other psychological superficialities, as if these antics will bring them to understand themselves more deeply and become more emotionally balanced. This approach may be, at the very least, misleading, and at worst, reflect an unconscious protest against the difficult work required for psychological change.

Deep psychological change is, regrettably, usually slow, time-consuming, and expensive. It involves a commitment to a potentially painful process of self-examination and the owning of emotional vulnerabilities that many of us are reluctant to undertake. It is a process that does not enhance the ego. Rather, it may require a conscious choice to sacrifice the supremacy of the ego. The "old king" cannot just don new garb, or the "wild man" a bearskin; he must die—and give birth to a new sense of Self. Relativizing the power of the ego means gaining access to the parts of personality that lie beneath the superficial layers of the personality. And this is where the inferior function plays such an important role in the eventual differentiation of the personality. As Marie-Louise von Franz, writes,

> The inferior function is the door through which all the figures of the unconscious come into consciousness. Our conscious realm is like a room with four doors, and it is the fourth door by which the Shadow, the Animus or the Anima and the personification of the Self come in. They do not enter as often through the other doors, which is in a way self-evident: the inferior function is so close to the unconscious and remains so barbaric and inferior and undeveloped that it is naturally the weak spot in consciousness through which the figures of the unconscious can break in. In consciousness it is experienced as a weak spot, as that disagreeable thing which will never leave one in peace and always causes trouble.[5]

The greatest difficulty for many men in really transforming themselves lies in the fact that what most needs changing often lies in the inferior function. Because it is opposite the dominant function, it is therefore the furthest away from consciousness. But the most undeveloped parts of ourselves often hold the solutions to many of our problems. Unlocking those parts can be the source of new energy and creative possibilities.

Most writers and researchers of typology think that it its practically impossible to make an "inferior function" conscious. Marie-Louise von Franz describes the inferior function as

> a horse that cannot be educated. It is something that can be subjugated to the extent that you do not do stupid things all the time. So much is possible. . . . You can never rule or educate it and make it act as you would like, but . . . you may be able to arrange so that it does not throw you.[6]

Or as Jung has pointed out:

> The essence of the inferior function is autonomy: it is independent, it attacks, it fascinates and so spins us about that we are no longer masters of ourselves and can no longer rightly distinguish between ourselves and others.[7]

Since the inferior function is so elusive, it is probably futile to try to approach it without first appealing to the auxiliary or the tertiary function.

For example, an extraverted thinking man, like Ted, might approach the inferior function through the secondary functions of sensation or intuition, since these functions have the possibility of being a little more developed and therefore more available. This is like approaching the unconscious sideways rather than head-on.

Ted had great difficulty in relating to his son Teddy with any real emotional depth. He felt embarrassed, awkward, and insincere when he tried to relate to him in less than an authoritative, paternal way. Yet, by using his "irrational" secondary functions (sensation and intuition) rather than his "rational" superior and inferior functions (thinking and feeling), he could be more supportive of Teddy and find new ways (intuition) to spend more time together. This might involve some practical activities (both have sensation) they would both enjoy. In this way Ted could begin, in an incremental way, to relate emotionally to Teddy. This would balance the part of their relationship in which Teddy was expected to fulfill his school responsibilities and to account to his father for his progress. It would allow a deeper feeling to develop naturally out of something mutually shared.

PSYCHOTHERAPY AS A VEHICLE FOR CHANGE

Most forms of psychotherapy are generally NF endeavors. In fact, the majority of clinical psychologists and psychiatrists are from the NF group. There are some important implications of this typological bias when we consider the difficulty most men have in allowing themselves to seek therapy. The fact that most psychotherapists are NF types and most men are ST types may unintentionally act to keep most men from seeking help.

Since so many men come from the ST group, they have a preexisting bias about the psychotherapy process itself. Because of the ST-NF opposition, there is also a natural shadow relationship between psychotherapists and the male population. The relational and communication styles of these two groups is even likely to create a natural psychological opposition between them. Many therapists and counselors intuitively know this, but may not adequately account for it in their practices.

For their part, psychotherapists naturally like to have their patients trust and believe in the processes with which they work. Too, male patients seeking help need to believe that what they are subjecting themselves to, and paying a lot of money for, is not only really going to help them, but will do so in ways they can readily understand. Because ST men often have a quantitative approach to life, they have a similar attitude toward therapy. They want to know how much it costs, how long it takes, what it does, and how it works. They don't like an approach that from their perspective takes a long time, is vague, and forces them to deal with underdeveloped parts of themselves. For the ST group, the functions most in need of understanding and developing are feeling and intuition, the very traits that are often dominant and naturally available in the therapist.

Thus, on the one hand, the very person the ST male patient needs is someone who has developed the functions that are troubling him. On the other hand, the therapist needs to understand that his or her own undeveloped functions are potentially the ones an ST patient has as dominants. While this introduces the possibility of help, it also introduces the potential for mutual shadow projection. Therefore it would be helpful for both to know that their strengths may be the other person's weaknesses. The potential bias can be reduced by an understanding of their differences. Without this knowledge therapy may turn out to be a brief and very disappointing affair for both of them. As an early ST patient of mine once said, "If I ran my office like you run this therapy, I'd be out of business." He was probably right since one could not easily run a business the way therapy is conducted. Of course, NFS are infrequently found among businessmen.

By its very nature, psychotherapy attempts to look beyond the merely physical (sensation) and logical (thinking) nature of human experience. Its "method" of understanding is rarely conveyed through the rational, cognitive style most men are accustomed to using. In a most general sense, a recurring goal in psychotherapy with men is the integration of their split-off feeling function with the thinking function. In that way it is more an affective or emotionally based process and it uses the opposite functions men are accustomed to using to solve problems.

For many women, psychotherapy is no less painful, but it is often more natural because its processes are those used by most women most of their lives. On the other hand, ST women often have many of the same difficulties with therapy that most men do. It is also harder for them to stay in treatment because they apply the same criteria their male counterparts do.

Men are frequently referred to therapy by physicians because the physical symptoms for which they sought medical attention turn out to have no organic basis. These men are puzzled, confused, and defensive when they are told that, physically, there is really nothing seriously wrong with them. They can't seem to understand how the mind and body work. It just doesn't make sense to them that the cause of pain in their bodies originated in their mind or feelings. In fact, ST men may need an extreme crisis or major illness to jolt them into looking inward, and certainly to ask someone else to help them do so.

A knowledge of typology can be helpful to men seeking therapy and for therapists who work with men. It helps both to understand why most men have so much difficulty in allowing themselves to seek help, particularly since emotional and psychological support seems both unacceptable and obscure to them.

In spite of the social and economic advantages males have traditionally enjoyed, they have been equally hurt by demands and expectations based on their unconscious adherence to sex roles. For example, social and familial expectations that men be emotionally strong, take care of themselves and their families, and act in nondependent ways deconditions them to accept help from others. So, the prospect of turning to another man or woman for "help" has very immediate negative overtones and goes directly against a large part of a societally imposed male image. As a result, many men are what I call "care-avoidant." Further, men's perception of the therapist is colored by a typological bias because the therapist is likely to be so "different" from themselves.[8] All of this may well account for the fact that 80 percent of those in therapy nationwide are women, and only 20 percent are men.

SUGGESTIONS FOR RAISING THE FEELING FUNCTION

A significant task for the collective consciousness of American men is to address our undeveloped feeling function. This is easier said than done and requires a commitment of emotional energy, risk, and most important, time. If we cultivate it, this elusive, largely unconscious function may reenter our awareness in a more deliberate way, eventually exerting a more conscious and positive effect on relationships and on the predominant values of our culture.

The prime area for men in which to consciously develop their feeling function is within their relationships. Here are some specific suggestions for ways men can develop better relationships through more conscious feeling. With sufficient motivation, anyone can do any of these things. All of these suggestions require investing time on a regular basis. Short of that, there will be no change.

In the father-son relationship:

1. Make an effort to deepen the emotional part of your relationships with your sons by allowing feeling to become a conscious part of the way you relate to them.

2. Become aware of whether your emotional responsiveness with your sons is more blunted than with your daughters.

3. Make time to talk openly with your sons about how they feel about school, their friends, their interests, and how they feel about you.

4. Ask your sons how they feel you could be a better dad, and what are the things they would like for the two of you to do together.

In friendships with other men:

1. If you don't have at least one close male friend, reach out to another man and ask to start a friendship. If this is difficult, ask yourself what feelings come up about it. Ask another man if he has similar feelings.

2. Make an effort to see that it is our childhood conditioning has made us afraid of intimacy with other men. Because of that we relate as if other men were our competitors and rivals. Discuss this with your friend.

3. Make a conscious attempt to spend quality time with a male friend, discussing more openly what you feel strongly about and why you *feel* that way, rather than only why you *think* that way. Ask him what he feels strongly about.

4. Talk with another man specifically about what frightens you about closeness to men.

5. Reach out physically to other men for hugs rather than distance-keeping handshakes. Hug your male friend goodbye, not just his wife. If this makes you uncomfortable, ask yourself what you would feel if you did reach out.

With wives, partners, and lovers:

1. Set aside some time each week to discuss what you liked about him or her that week.
2. Discuss something you would like to change about yourself in your relationship to your partner.
3. Discuss something you would rather not talk about.
4. Discuss a place you might like to go for a short trip together, then plan it.
5. Discuss some aspect of sex that makes you uncomfortable to think about.
6. Practice "active listening" once a week by having a short topic to discuss and give each other fifteen minutes of time to talk about it without interruption. Try to repeat back for five minutes what you thought your partner *felt* about what they were saying.
7. Spend fifteen minutes each week holding each other without talking or sex. Think about what that was like.
8. Discuss something that makes you feel vulnerable or inadequate.

With yourself:

1. Spend fifteen minutes a day learning a relaxation technique and see if you can keep your mind quiet during that time. If you can't, see what feelings come up for you.
2. Try to remember your dreams. Keep a pencil by your bedside and if you wake with a dream write it down. Ask yourself what feelings came up in the dream. If there were no feelings, ask yourself what you *would have felt* if the dream actually happened. Dreams often bring feelings we need to be having but won't let ourselves have consciously.
3. Ask yourself each morning if there is something you should be doing to make your life more comfortable, more

healthy, or more enjoyable. Make a sincere effort to do what is needed. If you resist doing what is needed, ask yourself why. If you still don't do what is needed, get some outside help to discuss your resistance.

About the world:

1. Ask yourself what is happening in the world, to the environment, or in politics that disturbs you. Ask yourself what your feelings are about that.

2. Ask yourself if there is some cause, concern, or issue you could take a more active role in.

3. Ask yourself if there is something you are personally capable of doing, reasonably within your means, to help someone less fortunate. Giving time to that might serve your personal development more than giving money.

If we can reown and develop our feeling in a renewed and more authentic way we can strengthen our relationships with others and improve the quality of our lives. Only by first nurturing feeling within will we be able to strengthen our relationships with our parents, children, women, other men, and the world.

As socially imposed sex roles increasingly lose their rigidity, both men and women may gain the freedom to develop and express more of their psychologically androgynous potential. As this happens we may find that the frequency of certain types among both men and women begins to change as a reflection of the lessened pressure to conform to stereotypical patterns of masculinity and femininity.

These changes will very likely decrease the tension between men and women created by the inequalities imposed by conventional sex-typed attitudes and communication styles reflected in their psychological type. And these changes may also increase options for equality in work, relationship, and family life for men and women. In this way, both men and woman may find more equitable and comfortable psychological, emotional, and social roles for themselves.

PSYCHOLOGICAL ANDROGYNY: THE FUTURE OF CONSCIOUSNESS?

The descriptive aspect of psychological type tells us that a good deal of the development of personality resides in the differentiation of at least one primary process of judging—either thinking or feeling—or a primary process of perception—sensation or intuition. The auxiliary or secondary function is thought to augment this primary process and to give the individual some access to the other pole of his attitude, either introversion or extraversion. In this paradigm, the tertiary and inferior functions are the "lost children" of the personality and rarely, if ever, grow up and amount to anything.

However, part of the beauty of typology as a system for understanding consciousness is its dynamic aspect, which involves raising and integrating the less developed functions. This is nowhere more clear than as it applies to the psychology of men and our need to raise the feeling function to greater consciousness. To neglect this need is to fail in the very task of psychological differentiation that typology offers. Without the differentiation of the feeling function, typology for men remains a static, merely descriptive device that, however academically or functionally interesting, has no potential benefit.

The descriptive aspect may well describe our present state of consciousness—where we have come from and where we are. But its greatest value lies in an implied direction for the future of consciousness, a direction that has everything to do with the practical way we live our lives—how we regard our partners, children, and other men. How we respect, regard, or even abuse our partners, how we approach and understand our children, or whether we should wage a war, have everything to do with the challenge and necessity of integrating thinking and feeling in consciousness.

Our world and lives are replete with demonstrations of the failure to integrate thinking and feeling. A particularly ironic and ludicrous example of thinking dissociated from feeling is apparent in recent discussions during the Persian Gulf War about whether women should be allowed the "right" to engage in active combat. One general's protest against giving this right to women was to remind us that "active combat is about killing people." How is it possible to consider the merits of whether women have the "right" to engage in active combat, and at the same time not even question whether men should be absolved of their presumed "obligation" to kill others in combat? Why is it that men's judgment rules questions involving women's welfare? Should a panel made up predominantly of women decide whether men should have the right to vasectomies? Why do so many people who support antiabortion legislation simultaneously endorse the death penalty? Why do religious bodies ruled by men decide that birth control is immoral, or non-Christian? All of these questions reflect a current state of consciousness not only dominated by sexist thinking but also unhampered by a integration of thinking and feeling.

When someone—either male or female—has developed the capacity for an easy interplay of both thinking and feeling processes, and with some depth, they are psychologically androgynous. The androgynous person relies on neither thinking nor feeling exclusively to evaluate experience and values. Their consciousness therefore becomes richer and more complex. Their identity is more whole, less simplistic, and more differentiated. Rigid personas, platitudes, moralisms, self-righteousness, and easy answers are unable to survive the task of differentiating not only how we both think *and* feel, but learning as well how to use feeling and thinking together as equivalent values.

In the psychological androgyne, intelligence becomes less of a learned skill and more a personal responsibility to understand the meaning and importance of the questions themselves, not just the "right" answers. For the androgyne, the questions themselves become more comprehensive, less easy to answer, but capable of producing more differentiated and humane values—among them more empathy, for ourselves as well as for others.

The reward of complexity is that the many sides of issues, values, and decisions can then be seen more completely. Personal decisions can then be seen more completely. Personal decisions about how one holds and lives out the specific values of one's life, what social and political ventures are supported or not, and the reasons *and* feelings for what one lives for become more clear.

Using thinking and feeling in tandem requires us to tease, pull, and tug at complexities that with only one function we are wont to forget and ignore. Engendering complexity by developing both the thinking and feeling functions—and using them—deepens one's values as well as one's experience.

Appendix

Table 1. The sixteen types and their order of preferences

TYPE	DOMINANT →	AUXILIARY →	TERTIARY →	INFERIOR
ESTJ	Thinking	Sensation	Intuitive	Feeling
ESTP	Sensation	Thinking	Feeling	Intuitive
ISTJ	Sensation	Thinking	Feeling	Intuition
ESFJ	Feeling	Sensation	Intuitive	Thinking
ESFP	Sensation	Feeling	Thinking	Intuitive
ENTP	Intuition	Thinking	Feeling	Sensation
ISTP	Thinking	Sensation	Intuition	Feeling
ENFP	Intuitive	Feeling	Thinking	Sensation
ENTJ	Thinking	Intuitive	Sensation	Feeling
ISFP	Feeling	Sensation	Intuition	Thinking
INTP	Thinking	Intuition	Thinking	Feeling
ISFJ	Sensation	Feeling	Thinking	Intuition
INTJ	Intuitive	Thinking	Feeling	Sensation
INFP	Feeling	Intuition	Sensation	Thinking
ENFJ	Feeling	Intuitive	Sensation	Thinking
INFJ	Intuitive	Feeling	Thinking	Sensation

Table 2. Distribution of preferences

E/I	Extraversion	70%
	Introversion	30%
S/N	Sensation	70%
	Intuition	30%
T/F	Thinking	
	male	65–70%
	female	30–35%
	Feeling	
	male	30–35%
	female	65–70%
J/P	Judging	60–65%
	Perceiving	35–40%

Table 3. Distribution between the sexes of the dominant function

Dominant Function		Males	Females
ET:	Extraverted Thinking	22%	15%
ES:	Extraverted Sensation	16%	16%
IS:	Introverted Sensation	13%	14%
EN:	Extraverted Intuition	12%	13%
EF:	Extraverted Feeling	11%	25%
IT:	Introverted Thinking	11%	4%
IF:	Introverted Feeling	9%	10%
IN:	Introverted Intuition	5%	3%

Table 4. Distribution between the sexes of the dominant and auxiliary functions

Dominant/Auxiliary Grouping	Males	Females
ST: Sensation Thinking	41%	23%
SF: Sensation Feeling	26%	47%
NT: Intuition Thinking	20%	9%
NF: Intuition Feeling	14%	20%

Table 5. Distribution between the sexes for groupings of combinations

Combinations	Males	Females
STJ: Sensation Thinking Judging	26%	17%
STP: Sensation Thinking Perceiving	15%	6%
SFJ: Sensation Feeling Judging	13%	30%
SFP: Sensation Feeling Perceiving	12%	17%
NTJ: Intuition Thinking Judging	9%	4%
NTP: Intuition Thinking Perceiving	11%	5%
NFJ: Intuition Feeling Judging	4%	6%
NFP: Intuition Feeling Perceiving	9%	14%

Table 6. Distribution of the Sixteen Types

Type and Male Portrayal		Males	Females
ESTJ:	Ted, bank officer	17%	13%
ESTP:	Jake, carpenter	9%	4%
ISTJ:	Richard, accountant	9%	5%
ESFJ:	Phil, teacher	8%	20%
ESFP:	Wally, stable owner	7%	12%
ENTP:	Paul, Cal's son	6%	3%
ISTP:	Harry, repairman	6%	2%
ENFP:	Jerry, youth group leader	6%	9%
ENTJ:	Sheldon, school administrator	5%	2%
ISFP:	Teddy, Ted's son	5%	6%
INTP:	Cal, math professor/Ted's brother	5%	2%
ISFJ:	Brian, family physician	4%	9%
INTJ:	Alexander, neuropsychologist	4%	1%
INFP:	Eliot, psychologist	3%	4%
ENFJ:	Pablo, church organist	3%	4%
INFJ:	Dean, minister	2%	2%

Table 7. Four communication styles

TJ types	SP types	FJ types	NP types
ESTJ	ESTP	ESFJ	ENTP
ISTJ	ISTP	ISFJ	INTP
ENTJ	ESFP	ENFJ	ENFP
INTJ	ISFP	INFJ	INFP
have thinking styles	have sensing styles	have feeling styles	have intuitive styles
35% of males 21% of females	28% of males 23% of females	17% of males 37% of females	21% of males 19% of females

Table 8. Communication styles of the ST group

ST Group "Thinkers"	Type	Dominant	Auxiliary	Communication Style
Ted	ESTJ	Ext. Thinking	Int. Sensation	Thinking
Shadow type: Pablo	*ENFJ*	*Ext. Feeling*	*Int. Intuition*	*Feeling*
Jake	ESTP	Ext. Sensation	Int. Thinking	Sensation
Shadow type: Jerry	*ENFP*	*Ext. Intuition*	*Int. Feeling*	*Intuition*
Richard	ISTJ	Int. Sensation	Ext. Thinking	Thinking
Shadow type: Eliot	*INFP*	*Int. Feeling*	*Ext. Intuition*	*Intuition*
Harry	ISTP	Int. Thinking	Ext. Sensation	Sensation
Shadow type: Dean	*INFJ*	*Int. Intuition*	*Ext. Feeling*	*Feeling*

Table 9. Communication styles of the NT group

NT Group "Idea Men"	Type	Dominant	Auxiliary	Communication Style
Sheldon	ENTJ	Ext. Thinking	Int. Intuition	Thinking
Shadow type: Phil	*ESFJ*	*Ext. Feeling*	*Int. Sensation*	*Feeling*
Paul	ENTP	Ext. Intuition	Int. Thinking	Intuition
Shadow type: Wally	*ESFP*	*Ext. Sensation*	*Int. Feeling*	*Sensation*
Alexander	INTJ	Int. Intuition	Ext. Thinking	Thinking
Shadow type: Teddy	*ISFP*	*Int. Feeling*	*Ext. Sensation*	*Sensation*
Cal	INTP	Int. Thinking	Ext. Intuition	Intuition
Shadow type: Brian	*ISFJ*	*Int. Sensation*	*Ext. Feeling*	*Feeling*

Table 10. Communication styles of the SF group

SF Group "Doers"	Type	Dominant	Auxiliary	Communication Style
Phil	ESFJ	Ext. Feeling	Int. Sensation	Feeling
Shadow type: Sheldon	*ENTJ*	*Ext. Thinking*	*Int. Intuition*	*Thinking*
Wally	ESFP	Ext. Sensation	Int. Feeling	Sensation
Shadow type: Paul	*ENTP*	*Ext. Intuition*	*Int. Thinking*	*Intuition*
Brian	ISFJ	Int. Sensation	Ext. Feeling	Feeling
Shadow type: Cal	*INTP*	*Int. Thinking*	*Ext. Intuition*	*Intuition*
Teddy	ISFP	Int. Feeling	Ext. Sensation	Sensation
Shadow type: Alexander	*INTJ*	*Int. Intuitive*	*Ext. Thinking*	*Thinking*

Table 11. Communication styles of the NF group

NF Group "Dreamers"	Type	Dominant	Auxiliary	Communication Style
Pablo	ENFJ	Ext. Feeling	Int. Intuition	Feeling
Shadow type: Ted	*ESTJ*	*Ext. Thinking*	*Int. Sensation*	*Thinking*
Jerry	ENFP	Ext. Intuition	Int. Feeling	Intuition
Shadow type: Jake	*ESTP*	*Ext. Sensation*	*Int. Thinking*	*Sensation*
Dean	INFJ	Int. Intuition	Ext. Feeling	Feeling
Shadow type: Harry	*ISTP*	*Int. Thinking*	*Ext. Sensation*	*Sensation*
Eliot	INFP	Int. Feeling	Ext. Intuition	Intuition
Shadow type: Richard	*ISTJ*	*Int. Sensation*	*Ext. Thinking*	*Thinking*

Table 12. Frequency of certain occupations: function and attitude preferences

Type	Psychologist	Manager	Mechanic	Engineer	Writer	Farmer	Policeman
E: I	51 : 49%	57 : 43%	50 : 50%	48 : 52%	53 : 47%	51 : 49%	49 : 50%
S: N	15 : 85%	56 : 43%	50 : 50%	64 : 36%	26 : 74%	76 : 24%	85 : 15%
T: F	45 : 55%	62 : 38%	53 : 47%	64 : 36%	43 : 57%	71 : 29%	68 : 32%
J: P	48 : 52%	70 : 30%	54 : 46%	60 : 40%	43 : 57%	58 : 42%	66 : 34%

Table 13. Frequency of certain occupations: ST, SF, NT, NF groupings

Type	Psychologist	Manager	Mechanic	Engineer	Writer	Farmer	Policeman
ST	8%	37%	38%	36%	13%	51%	57%
SF	7%	19%	28%	16%	13%	25%	28%
NT	37%	24%	15%	27%	30%	19%	11%
NF	48%	20%	20%	20%	44%	4%	4%

Table 14. Frequency of certain occupations: the sixteen types

Type	Psychol-ogist	Manager	Mechanic	Engineer	Writer	Farmer	Police Officer
ESTJ	3%	17%	13%	12%	5%	19%	22%
ESTP	0.5%	3%	4%	4%	3%	7%	8%
ISTJ	3%	15%	12%	15.5%	4%	15%	21%
ESFJ	2%	7%	7.5%	5%	3.5%	7%	8%
ESFP	1%	3%	0.5%	3%	4%	6%	3%
ENTP	6%	5%	0.5%	6%	7%	7%	4.5%
ISTP	1.5%	3%	0.8%	5%	1%	10%	6%
ENFP	18%	7%	0.8%	7%	17%	0%	1%
ENTJ	12%	10%	0.4%	7.5%	5%	6%	1%
ISFP	1%	2.5%	5.5%	2.5%	2%	4%	6%
INTP	8%	4%	2.5%	6%	9%	4%	3%
ISFJ	2.5%	6%	9%	6%	4%	8%	10%
INTJ	11%	6%	3%	8%	8.5%	3%	2%
INFP	15%	5%	6.5%	6%	14%	4%	0.6%
ENFJ	8%	5%	3%	4%	9%	0%	1%
INFJ	7%	3%	2%	3%	4%	0%	0.6%

Note: Statistics in tables were summarized from Isabel Briggs Myers and Mary H. McCaulley, *Manual: A Guide to the Development and the Use of the Myers-Briggs Type Indicator,* and from Mary H. McCaulley, Gerald P. Macdaid, and Richard I. Kainz, "Estimated Frequencies of the MBTI Types." See the bibliography for cite information.

Notes

In the notes, CW refers to *The Collected Works of C. G. Jung,* 20 vols. (Princeton: Princeton University Press, 1967–1978).

Introduction

1. Ted Guzie and Noreen Monroe Guzie. "Masculine and Feminine Archetypes: A Complement to the Psychological Types." *Journal of Psychological Type* 7 (1984): 3–11.
2. Katherine Bradway and Wayne Detloff. "Incidence of Psychological Types among Jungian Analysts Classified by Self and by Test." *Journal of Analytical Psychology* 21 (1976): 134–46.

Chapter 1. What Is Typology?

1. C. G. Jung, *Psychological Types,* CW 6, p. xi, italics added.
2. According to Marie-Louise von Franz, Jung's own dominant function in the circle was that of an introverted thinking type, while Freud's was that of introverted feeling. See *G. G. Jung: His Myth in Our Time* (Boston & Ontario: Little, Brown and Co., 1975), p. 61.
3. C. G. Jung, *Two Essays on Analytical Psychology,* CW 7, pp. 43–44.

4. Isabel Briggs Myers, *Introduction to Type* (Palo Alto, Calif.: Consulting Psychologists Press, Inc., 1987), p. 5.
5. C. G. Jung, *The Symbolic Life,* CW 18, p. 12.
6. Ibid.
7. Isabel Briggs Myers, *Introduction to Type* (Palo Alto, Calif.: Consulting Psychologists Press, Inc., 1987), p. 5.
8. Jung, *The Symbolic Life,* CW 18, pp. 14–15.
9. Isabel Briggs Myers, *Introduction to Type* (Palo Alto, Calif.: Consulting Psychologists Press, Inc., 1987), p. 5.
10. This favoring of sensation was in large part based on psychology's early need to justify itself as a legitimate scientific discipline alongside the other "hard" sciences. Throughout the history of psychology, there have been serious and unfortunate consequences of this effort. One of the most notable examples is the rise of behaviorism in the 1940s and '50s with its rigid reliance on only the measurable qualities of behavior. Behaviorism largely ignored the field of perception; mental experiences like intuition, imagination, and creativity were particularly dismissed as "unscientific" because they were not measurable. This resulted in a decidedly masculine bias within psychology. It was not until the early 1970s that these ostracized mental processes were able to return with some respect. They have increasingly become regarded as not only useful, but essential to understanding the breadth and depth of human experience.
11. Jung, *The Symbolic Life,* CW 18, p. 12.
12. Isabel Briggs Myers, *Introduction to Type* (Palo Alto, California: Consulting Psychologists Press, Inc., 1987), p. 6.
13. C. G. Jung, *The Symbolic Life,* CW 18, p. 13.
14. Isabel Briggs Myers, *Introduction to Type* (Palo Alto, California: Consulting Psychologists Press, Inc., 1987), p. 6.
15. Daryl Sharp, *Personality Types: Jung's Model of Typology* (Toronto: Inner City Books, 1987), p. 16.
16. Isabel Briggs Myers, *Gifts Differing* (Palo Alto, Calif.: Consulting Psychologists Press, 1987), pp. 12–13.

17. Angelo Spoto, *Jung's Typology In Perspective* (Boston: Sigo Press, 1989), p. 53.
18. This notion of bipolarity has been questioned by June Singer and Mary Loomis in their own type research (see Loomis and Singer in the bibliography). The questions in the Singer-Loomis Inventory of Personality (SLIP) allow for a free choice of the function and type attitude rather than the forced choice method of the questions of other type tests. John Beebe, an analyst from San Francisco, reaffirms the bipolar nature of the functions as well as of the type attitude, based on his own clinical observations of type.

Chapter 2. Psychological Type and the Ways Men Communicate

1. Quoted in Deborah Tannen, *You Just Don't Understand: Men and Women in Conversation* (New York: Ballantine, 1990), pp. 229–31. See also Jack Sattel, "Men, Inexpressiveness, and Power," in *Language, Gender, and Society,* Barrie Thorne, Cherris Kramarae, and Nancy Henley, eds. (Rowley, Mass.: Newberry House, 1983), pp. 119–24.
2. Barbara Eakins and Gene Eakins, *Sex Differences in Human Communication* (Boston: Houghton Mifflin Company, 1978), pp. 48–51.
3. Flavil Yeakley, "Communication Style Preferences and Adjustments as an Approach to Studying Effects of Similarity in Psychological Type," *Research in Psychological Type* 6 (1983): 23.
4. Ibid., pp. 22–33.

Chapter 3. The Thinkers

1. Mary H. McCaulley, Gerald P. Macdaid, Richard I. Kainz, "Estimated Frequencies of the MBTI Types," *Journal of Psychological Type* 9 (1985): 3–9.
2. Myers, *Gifts Differing,* p. 158.
3. Isabel Briggs Myers and Mary H. McCaulley, *Manual: A Guide to the Development and the Use of the Myers-Briggs*

Type Indicator (Palo Alto, Calif.: Consulting Psychologists Press, 1985), p. 33.

4. Siegler M. Mann and H. Osmond, "The Many Worlds of Time," *Journal of Analytical Psychology* 13 (1968): 35–56.

5. Myers, *Gifts Differing*, p. 158.

Chapter 4. The Idea Men

1. Mann and Osmond, "The Many Worlds of Time," pp. 33–56.

2. Myers and McCaulley, *Manual: A Guide to the Development and the Use of the Myers-Briggs Type Indicator*, p. 35.

Chapter 5. The Doers

1. Myers and McCaulley, *Manual: A Guide to the Development and the Use of the Myers-Briggs Type Indicator*, p. 34.

2. Mann and Osmond, "The Many Worlds of Time," pp. 33–56.

3. Myers, *Gifts Differing*, p. 158.

Chapter 6. The Dreamers

1. Myers and McCaulley, *Manual: A Guide to the Development and the Use of the Myers-Briggs Type Indicator*, p. 35.

2. Mann and Osmond, "The Many Worlds of Time," pp. 33–56.

3. By referring to table 12 in the appendix we can see how the frequency of various components of type exert a powerful effect on choice of occupation. For example, intuition alone is a deciding factor in the choice of careers involving both psychology and writing. The intuitive function occurs in 85 percent of psychologists and 74 percent of writers. All of the other elements of type are nearly equally distributed in these two occupations, except feeling, which is favored somewhat more by both of them over thinking. On the other hand, police officers have almost the opposite configuration: they favor sensation (85 percent) to intuition (15 percent). On the thinking-feeling polarity, police officers are again opposite, favoring thinking (68 percent) to feeling (32 percent).

4. Myers, *Gifts Differing*, p. 96.

Chapter 7. Using Typology as a Psychology of Consciousness

1. Arthur Colman and Libby Colman, *The Father: Mythology and Changing Roles* (Wilmette, Ill.: Chiron Publications, 1988), p. 34.

2. Jung defines the feeling function this way:

> Feeling is primarily a process that takes place between the *ego* . . . and a given content, a process, moreover, that imparts to the content a definite *value* in the sense of acceptance or rejection ("like" or "dislike"). The process can also appear isolated, as it were, in the form of a "mood," regardless of the momentary contents of consciousness or momentary sensations. The mood may be causally related to earlier conscious contents, though not necessarily so, since, as psychopathology amply proves, it may equally well arise from unconscious contents. But even a mood, whether it be a general or only a partial feeling, implies a valuation; not of one definite, individual conscious content, but of the whole conscious situation at the moment, and, once again, with special reference to the question of acceptance or rejection. (Jung, *Psychological Types,* CW 6, para. 724)

3. Marie-Louise von Franz and James Hillman, *Lectures on Jung's Typology* (New York: Spring Publications, 1971), p. 19.

4. In a study reported by Isabel Briggs Myers that was done almost fifty years ago, it was found that when extraverts marry they tend to reduce the degree of thinking-feeling oppositeness.

> Where the man was an extravert, 62 percent of the couples were alike on T-F; where he was an introvert, 49 percent were alike. Where husband and wife were both extraverts, the similarity on T-F rose to 66 percent, which is high considering that the maximum possible was only 78 percent.

While this study is an old one, it is one of the few with such a large sample size and likely has a good deal of validity even in the present. The effect of decreasing rigidity of sex roles may have the effect of increasing similarity of types in marriage for both introverts and extraverts. Myers, *Gifts Differing,* p. 132.

5. Von Franz and Hillman, *Lectures on Jung's Typology,* p. 54.
6. Von Franz and Hillman, *Lectures on Jung's Typology,* p. 19.
7. Jung, *Two Essays on Analytical Psychology,* CW 7, para. 85.
8. There are some fascinating differences between men of the different type groups in terms of their interest in therapy, counseling, and other avenues to resolving psychological problems and increasing self-awareness. The STs tend to be the least naturally interested in these processes. For example, a group of medical students was asked, "How important is it for the faculty to help you with your own personal development and self-understanding?" ST types expressed low interest, reporting that the faculty already emphasized it more than they wanted. NF types, on the other hand, reported high interest in self-understanding, feeling that the faculty was neglecting this part of their education.

For NFs, dreams, fantasies, and myths are realities that help explain the different dimensions of life. They often take to analysis and therapy with an almost natural sense of comfort. In fact, many of the NF analysands I have seen over the years have gone on to become therapists themselves. Some studies of type and therapy have shown that NFs, and particularly introverts, are likely to come more frequently for counseling as well as to stay longer in treatment. The majority of the men I see in analysis are of the NF or NT orientation (this is also true of women in analysis).

A number of NF men come to analysis in their later years in order to deepen their understanding of themselves, even though they might not feel that they have specific psychological troubles. What they seem to want is more from life than the materialism of the outer world has had to offer. As they grow older, they long for deeper emotional and spiritual fulfillment.

On the other hand, ST men may need an extreme crisis or major illness to jolt them into looking inward. Ordinarily their psyches seem abstract, diffuse, confusing, and unavailable to them. They apply criteria to therapy they use in the outer world of work, finances, and business. *They want to know how long therapy will take, what's expected of them, what they need to "do," and whether or not it really "works."* They try to focus on the factual aspects of self-awareness, trusting more the objective analysis of the problems they face. Since they want verification of facts through their senses, inner psychological work may seem fuzzy and "ungraspable" to them. *ST men may become psychologists, but they are often more interested in experimental and physiological psychology than in working directly with people.*

The SF group, like the STs, prefer sensation but rely more on the feeling function to determine their interests and pursuits. They occupy a middle ground between the NFs and the STs because, like the STs, they are interested in facts; however, they are more interested in how these facts are related to other people or to themselves.

The majority of mental health workers have type cores of NF and NT. Intuition, with its perceptive regard for possibilities rather than facts, is perhaps the most "psychologically" oriented function of typology. Like the NFs, the NTs (especially when intuition is dominant), may also be deeply responsive to the psyche and its myriad possibilities, but (when thinking is dominant) they may prefer even greater objectivity, and hence be more oriented to psychology as a science. NFs are more the "artists" of therapy, NTs more often the scientists.

Of course, there is nothing absolute about any of these generalizations. What I am attempting to portray is a general schematic outline to show some of the ways different type dispositions relate to the processes of self-awareness and the development of consciousness.

Glossary

Included with some of the definitions given here are references to either C. G. Jung's *Collected Works,* vols. 6 or 7, or Isabel Briggs Myers's and Mary H. McCaulley's *Manual: A Guide to the Development and Use of the Myers-Briggs Type Indicator.* in the former case the reference is given by indicating the volume and paragraph of the *Collected Works,* e.g., CW 6, para. 681; in the latter, the reference is simply designated by *Manual* and the page number. See the bibliography for cite information.

Affect

Jung defines affect as "A state of feeling characterized by marked physical innervation on the one hand and a peculiar disturbance of the ideational process on the other. I use *emotion* as synonymous with affect. I distinguish . . . *feeling* . . . from affect, in spite of the fact that the dividing line is fluid, since every feeling, after attaining a certain strength, releases physical innervations, thus becoming an affect. For practical reasons, however, it is advisable to distinguish affect from feeling, since feeling can be a voluntarily disposable function, whereas affect is usually not. Similarly, affect is clearly distinguished from feeling by quite perceptible physical innervations, while feeling for the most part lacks them, or else their intensity is so slight. . . . I regard affect on the one hand as a psychic feeing-state and on the other as a physiological innervation-state, each of which has a cumulative, reciprocal effect on the other." (CW 6, para. 681)

Anima

Jung called the feminine representations for a man's unconscious the *anima*. This contrasexual component in men occurs in the form of feminine images. These images can be found in men's dreams, fantasies, and in their projections onto real women. "The soul-image is a specific image among those produced by the unconscious. . . . Sometimes these images are of quite unknown or mythological figures. With men the anima is usually personified by the unconscious as a woman." (CW 6, para. 808)

Archetype

Archetypes are primordial representations of the collective unconscious found across many divergent cultures. The archetypes may be represented by mythological images having a numinous quality. Since they are at the core of complexes, they influence certain patterns of behavior. When they are experienced, they provide a source of psychic energy capable of catalyzing consciousness.

Attitude

The orientation of extraversion (E) or introversion (I). In the extraverted attitude, libido or attention flows out to the objects and people of the environment and away from the subject. In the introverted attitude, energy is withdrawn from the environment and is directed inward toward the subject. All functions can be either extraverted or introverted.

Auxiliary Function

A secondary process sufficiently differentiated to provide complementary balance to the dominant function. If the dominant process is a judging process, the auxiliary will be a perceiving process. If the dominant process is a perceiving process, the auxiliary will be a judging process.

For extraverts, because the dominant process is extraverted, the auxiliary process looks after their inner lives; for introverts, because the dominant process is introverted, the auxiliary process functions for them in the outer world.

Communication Style

A particular style in which contents of a communication are conveyed or expressed by one's psychological type. The nucleus of the type determines the specific style; extraverts primarily use their dominant function to convey that style, and introverts use their auxiliary function.

Complex

Jung described the complex as a feeling-toned image which, with respect to the ego, was autonomous and capable of manifesting at the least provocation. When the complex is activated it takes over the sphere of consciousness, causing an individual to feel "taken over" by a force from outside of himself.

"[Complexes are] psychic entities which are outside the control of the conscious mind. They have been split off from consciousness and lead a separate existence in the dark realm of the unconscious, being at all times ready to hinder or reinforce the conscious functioning.

"[C]omplexes always contain something like a conflict, or at least are either the cause or the effect of a conflict. . . . They always contain memories, wishes, fears, duties, needs, or insights which somehow we can never really grapple with, and for this reason they constantly interfere with our conscious life in a disturbing and usually a harmful way. . . . It only means that something discordant, unassimilated, and antagonistic exists, perhaps as an obstacle, but also as an incentive to greater effort, and so, perhaps, to new possibilities of achievement." (CW 6, paras. 923–925)

Consciousness

In the context of typology, consciousness is described as the way in which the individual perceives and judges his or her experiences. By developing a capacity for differentiated perceptions and judgments, we improve the quality of consciousness.

"By consciousness I understand the relation of psychic contents to the *ego* . . . in so far as this relation is perceived as such by the ego. Relations to the ego that are not perceived as such are *unconscious*. . . . Consciousness is the function or activity which maintains the relation of psychic contents to the ego." (CW 6, para. 700)

Countertransference

The thoughts, feelings, and projections the analyst or therapist has in regard to the patient that are derived from his own personality or psychological background. These may be legitimate reactions to the patient (concordant countertransference) or derivatives mainly from the therapist's own unresolved complexes (neurotic countertransference).

Differentiated

A psychological function that is differentiated means that one is able to consciously understand, separate, and use that function as distinct from others. Differentiation "is the essence, the *sine qua non* of consciousness." (CW 7, para. 329)

Jung also wrote that "Differentiation means the development of differences, the separation of parts from a whole. In this work I employ the concept of differentiation chiefly with respect to the psychological functions." (CW 6, para. 705)

Dominant Function

One of the four functions (either a perceiving process or a judging process) that is the favored, most differentiated, and most trusted; the unifying force in a person's conscious personality. The other functions are subordinate to and serve the goals of the dominant function. For extraverts, the dominant function is concerned with the outer world of people and things; for introverts, the dominant function is engrossed with the inner world of ideas.

Ego

The center of consciousness. The source of conscious will and memory. The ego is most often related to one's personal sense of identity and reality testing.

"By ego I understand a complex of ideas which constitutes the centre of my field of consciousness and appears to possess a high degree of continuity and identity. Hence I also speak of an *ego-complex*. The ego-complex is as much a content as a condition of *consciousness*, . . . for a psychic element is conscious to me only in so far as it is related to my ego-complex. But inasmuch as the ego is only the centre of my field of consciousness, it is not identical with the totality of my psyche, being merely one complex among other complexes. I therefore distinguish between the ego and the self, since the ego is only the subject of my consciousness, while the self is the subject of my total psyche, which also includes the unconscious. In this sense the self would be an ideal entity which embraces the ego."(CW 6, para. 706)

Extraversion (E)

As described by Jung, extraversion is "an outward-turning of libido." In the extraverted attitude, libido or attention flows out to the objects and people of the environment and away from the subject. Preferred extraversion refers to a primary orientation toward the outer world where perception and judgment is focused on people and objects. (CW 6, para. 710)

Feeling (F)

One of the two rational or judging functions. A process of judging by which one comes to decisions based primarily on subjective values and merits of issues of personal concern. The feeling function seeks rational order according to harmony among personal and social values and imparts a value in the sense of acceptance or rejection.

Myers and McCaulley characterize those who have extraverted feeling as "sociable, friendly, and sympathetic. They like to make things happen for the pleasure or welfare of others." Those with introverted feeling "are quiet and caring. They have concern for deep and enduring values, as well as for people." (*Manual*, p. 38)

Function

By function Jung meant "a particular form of psychic activity that remains the same in principle under varying conditions," distinguishing four basic functions, two irrational (sensation and intuition) and two rational (thinking and feeling). The four functions or processes represent an individual's conscious orientation. These combine to produce sixteen types, which differ in the priorities they give to each function and in the attitudes (introversion and extraversion)." (CW 6, para. 731)

Individuality

"By individuality I mean the peculiarity and singularity of the individual in every psychological respect. Everything that is not *collective* . . . is individual, everything in fact that pertains only to one individual and not to a larger group of individuals. Individuality can hardly be said to pertain to the psychic elements themselves, but only to their peculiar and unique grouping and combination." (CW 6, para. 756)

Individuation

Psychological type plays a role in the individuation process by helping the individual to first both understand and strengthen the conscious attitude. With this understanding and strength he is prepared to explore and integrate the less conscious parts of his personality.

"The concept of individuation plays a large role in our psychology. In general, it is the process by which individual beings are formed and differentiated; in particular, it is the development of the psychological *individual* . . . as a being distinct from the general, collective psychology. Individuation, therefore, is a process of *differentiation,* . . . having for its goal the development of the individual personality." (CW 6, para. 757)

Inferior Function

The function that is the least differentiated, least trusted, and least conscious. It is opposite in every way to one's dominant function. Jung describes it as "the function that lags behind in the process of *differentiation* (CW 6, para. 763)."

Introversion (I)

In the introverted attitude, energy is withdrawn from the environment and is directed inward toward the subject. Preferred introversion refers to a primary orientation toward the inner world of concepts and ideas. As Jung states, introversion means "an inward-turning of libido (CW 6, para. 769)."

Intuition (N)

One of the two irrational or perceiving functions. A process of perceiving that reports meanings, relationships, and possibilities beyond what is visible to the senses and the conscious mind. Intuition seeks insight and possibilities.

Myers and McCaulley describe those with extraverted intuition as "change agents; they see possibilities as challenges to make something happen. They have wide-ranging interests and like to see new patterns and relationships." Those with introverted intuition "are introspective and scholarly. They are interested in knowledge for its own sake, as well as ideas, theory, and depth of understanding." (*Manual*, p. 37)

Irrational Functions

The perceiving functions of sensation (S) and intuition (N). They are called irrational because they are not concerned with reasoning.

Judging Functions

The two processes of judgment are thinking (T) and feeling (F). Judgment involves coming to conclusions: evaluating, making decisions about, and responding to what has been perceived.

Judgment (J)

The JP index refers to one's style of dealing with the outside world, favoring judgment (J) or perception (P). Judging types spend less time in the perceiving mode than perceiving types before reaching conclusions.

Perceiving Functions

Perception involves information gathering: selecting stimuli (things, people, happenings, or ideas) to attend to.

The two processes of perception are sensation (S) and intuition (N). These are called the irrational functions because as processes they do not involve evaluation.

Perception (P)

The JP index refers to one's style of dealing with the outside world, favoring judgment (J) or perception (P). Perceiving types remain longer in the perceiving mode than judging types before reaching conclusions.

Persona

Persona is a term from early drama meaning "mask." Psychologically it refers to the outermost layer of the personality, which is largely socially defined. When the persona is used simply to facilitate social and professional interactions, it helps the individual adapt to societal roles. If a person becomes identified with the persona, there is a loss of individuality as well as a loss of connection to the unconscious.

"The persona . . . largely consists of collective material inasmuch as the persona represents a compromise with society, the ego identifying more with the persona than with individuality. The more the ego identifies with the persona, the more the subject becomes what he appears to be, and is de-individualized. . . . When the ego is completely identical with the persona, individuality is wholly repressed, and the entire conscious psyche becomes collective. This represents the maximum adaptation to society and the minimum adaptation to one's own individuality." (CW 7, para. 518)

Projection

"Projection means the expulsion of a subjective content into an object; it is the opposite of *introjection*. . . . Accordingly, it is a process of *dissimilation*, . . . by which a subjective content becomes alienated from the subject and is, so to speak, embodied in the object. The subject gets rid of painful, incompatible contents by projecting them, as also of positive values which, for one reason or another— self-deprecation, for instance—are inaccessible to him." (CW 6, para. 783)

Psychological Type

"According to theory, by definition, one pole of each of the four preferences is preferred over the other pole for each of the sixteen MBTI types. . . . Each type has its own pattern of dominant and auxiliary processes and the attitudes (E or I) in which these are habitually used).

"The indices EI, SN, TF, JP reflect a habitual choice between rival alternatives. . . . Every person is assumed to use both poles of each of the four preferences, but to respond first or most often with the preferred functions or attitudes." (*Manual*, pp. 2–3)

Rational Functions

The judging functions of thinking (T) and feeling (F). They are called rational because they are concerned with reasoning.

Relational Style

While communication styles convey content, a relational style conveys the *impact* of the communication style on the listener.

Sensation (S)

One of the two irrational or perceiving functions. A process of perceiving that reports observable facts through one or more of the five senses, establishing what exists concretely in the immediate environment and in the present moment. Sensation seeks experience and reality.

Myers and McCaulley describe those with extraverted sensation as "active, realistic doers. Ess are the most practical of the types. They learn best when useful applications are obvious." Those with introverted sensation "like to test ideas to see whether they are supported by facts. They like to deal with what is real and factual in a careful, unhurried way." (*Manual,* p. 37)

Shadow

A psychic content which was once conscious but is split off because of its unacceptability to the ego. In other words, a part of ourselves from which we need to disidentify. These contents do not remain static, as they usually become a large part of what we project onto others.

Tertiary Function

This function is opposite to the auxiliary function. Although it is considered to be more accessible than the inferior function, it is often relatively undifferentiated.

Thinking (T)

One of the two rational or judging functions. A process of judging by which one comes to decisions based primarily on logical connections, principles of cause and effect. The thinking function seeks rational order according to impersonal logic and evaluates in a sense of true or false.

Myers and McCaulley describe those with extraverted thinking as "active and energetic. They are objective, and they like to make things happen in reasoned, analytical, and logical ways." Those with introverted thinking "are quiet and contemplative. They have concern for basic principles that explain the causes and consequences of events or the workings of things." (*Manual*, p. 38)

Transcendent Function

The capacity of the psyche to produce symbols which have the effect of synthesizing or unifying something previously psychologically or emotionally incompatible, or seemingly irreconcilable. As Jung writes, "I have called this process . . . the *transcendent function*, "function" being here understood not as a basic function but as a complex function made up of other functions, and "transcendent" not as denoting a metaphysical quality but merely the fact that this function facilitates a transition from one attitude to another. The raw material shaped by thesis and antithesis, and in the shaping of which the opposites are united, is the living symbol. Its profundity of meaning is inherent in the raw material itself, the very stuff of the psyche, transcending time and dissolution; and its configuration by the opposites ensures its sovereign power over all the psychic functions." (cw 6, para. 828)

Transference

A patient's thoughts, feelings, or complexes projected onto a therapist. These often represent the patient's developmental issues or derivatives of his early life experience.

Turntype

Some individuals behave as if they are a particular psychological type, but are only playing out an adaptation of that type. For different reasons these individuals were not free to develop psychologically along the lines of their natural disposition. A confusion of type due to a developmental interference with type development.

Unconscious

Freud described the unconscious as consisting of all of the repressed, suppressed, or forgotten material from conscious life. For Jung, in addition to Freud's "personal unconscious," there also exists a "collective unconscious" containing images, symbols, and mythic themes common to humanity. These collective representations are archetypal motifs found in the dreams, fantasies, and myths that span many cultures.

"The concept of the *unconscious* is for me an *exclusively psychological* concept, and not a philosophical concept of a metaphysical nature. In my view the unconscious is a psychological borderline concept, which covers all psychic contents or processes that are not conscious, i.e., not related to the *ego* . . . in any perceptible way." (CW 6, para. 837)

Undifferentiated Function

We say that one or more of the psychological functions is "undifferentiated" when it cannot be used independently from the other functions of consciousness. For example, a thinking type may be intelligent but unable to draw on his feeling function to counterbalance his tendency to be only impersonally objective or overly factual.

"So long as a function is still so fused with one or more other functions—thinking with feeling, feeling with sensation, etc.—that it is unable to operate on its own, it is in an *archaic* . . . condition, i.e., not differentiated, not separated from the whole as a special part and existing by itself. . . . As a rule, the undifferentiated function is also characterized by ambivalence and ambitendency, i.e., every position entails its own negation, and this leads to characteristic inhibitions in the use of the undifferentiated function." (CW 6, para. 705)

Bibliography

Bates, Marilyn, and David W. Keirsey. *Please Understand Me*. Del Mar, Calif.: Prometheus Nemesis Book Company, 1978.

Beebe, John. "Psychological Types in Transference, Countertransference, and the Therapeutic Interaction." *Chiron: A Review of Jungian Analysis*, 1984: 147–61.

Bennet, E. A. *What Jung Really Said*. New York: Shocken Books, 1967.

Bisbee, Cynthia, Robert Mullaly, and Humphry Osmond. "Type and Psychiatric Illness." *Research in Psychological Type* 5 (1982): 49–68.

Bradway, Katherine, and Wayne Detloff. "Incidence of Psychological Types among Jungian Analysts Classified by Self and by Test." *Journal of Analytical Psychology* 21 (1976): 134–46.

Chinen, Allan B., Anne Spielvogel, and Dennis Farrell. "The Experience of Intuition." *Psychological Perspectives* 16, no. 2 (1985): 186–97.

Colman, Arthur, and Libby Colman. *The Father: Mythology and Changing Roles*. Wilmette, Ill.: Chiron Publications, 1988.

Eakins, Barbara Westbrook, and R. Gene Eakins. *Sex Differences in Human Communication*. Boston: Houghton Mifflin Company, 1978.

Ekstrom, S. R. "Jung's Typology and DSM-III Personality Disorders: A Comparison of Two Systems of Classification." *Journal of Analytical Psychology* 33 (1988): 329–44.

Frank, Robert H. *Passions Within Reason: The Strategic Role of the Emotions.* New York and London: W. W. Norton, 1988.

Grant, Harold W., Magdala Thompson, and Thomas E. Clarke. *From Image to Likeness: A Jungian Path in the Gospel Journey.* New York: Paulist Press, 1983.

Guzie, Ted, and Noreen Monroe Guzie. "Masculine and Feminine Archetypes: A Complement to the Psychological Types." *Journal of Psychological Type* 7 (1984): 3–11.

Hammer, Allen L. "Type and Coping Resources." Paper presented at the Bay Area Association of Psychological Type. Stanford University, Palo Alto, Calif., 1991.

Hirsch, Sandra, and Jean Kummerow. *Lifetypes.* New York: Warner Books, 1989.

Hobson, Robert F. *Forms of Feeling: The Heart of Psychotherapy.* London and New York: Tavistock Publications, 1985.

Jung, C. G. *Memories, Dreams, Reflections.* Recorded and edited by Aniela Jaffé. Translated by Richard and Clara Winston. New York: Pantheon Books, 1961.

————. *Psychological Types.* Translated by R. F. C. Hull. Bollingen Series XX. *Collected Works,* vol. 6. Princeton: Princeton University Press, 1971.

————. *The Symbolic Life.* Translated by R. F. C. Hull. Bollingen Series XX. *Collected Works,* vol. 18. Princeton: Princeton University Press, 1976.

————. *Two Essays on Analytical Psychology.* Second ed. Translated by R. F. C. Hull. Bollingen Series XX. *Collected Works,* vol. 7. Princeton: Princeton University Press, 1966.

Keirsey, David. *Portraits of Temperament.* Del Mar, Calif.: Prometheus Nemesis Book Company, 1978.

Key, Mary Ritchie. *Male/Female Language.* Metuchen, N.J.: Scarecrow Press, 1975.

————. *Paralanguage and Kinesics (Nonverbal Communication).* Metuchen: N.J.: Scarecrow Press, 1975.

Kroeger, Otto, and Janet M. Thuesen. *Typetalk.* New York: Delacorte Press, 1988.

Lambert, Kenneth. *Analysis, Repair and Individuation. The Library of Analytical Psychology,* vol. 5. Edited by Michael Fordham, et al. London: Academic Press, 1981.

Lawrence, Gordon. *People Types and Tiger Stripes.* Gainesville, Fla.: Center for the Application of Psychological Type, 1982.

Mann, Siegler M., and H. Osmond. "The Many Worlds of Time." *Journal of Analytical Psychology* 13 (1968): 33–56.

McCaulley, Mary H., Gerald P. Macdaid, and Richard I. Kainz. "Estimated Frequencies of the MBTI Types." *Journal of Psychological Type* 9 (1985): 3–9.

Meier, C. A. *Consciousness.* Translated by David N. Roscoe. Boston: Sigo Press, 1989.

Merner, Murray H., and Thomas G. Carskadon. "Partner Similarity on the Myers-Briggs Type Indicator Among Functional and Dysfunctional Married Couples." *Research In Psychological Type* 6 (1983): 76–80.

Myers, Isabel Briggs. *Introduction to Type.* Rev. ed. Palo Alto, Calif.: Consulting Psychologists Press, 1987.

Myers, Isabel Briggs, and Mary H. McCaulley. *Manual: A Guide to the Development and Use of the Myers-Briggs Type Indicator.* Palo Alto, Calif.: Consulting Psychologists Press, 1985.

Myers, Isabel Briggs. *Gifts Differing.* Palo Alto, Calif.: Consulting Psychologists Press, 1980.

Newman, James. *A Cognitive Perspective on Jungian Typology.* Gainesville, Fla.: Center for Applications of Psychological Type, 1990.

Padgett, Valerie R., David D. Cook, Michael E. Nunley, and Thomas G. Carskadon. "Psychological Type, Androgyny, and Sex-typed Roles." *Research in Psychological Type* 5 (1982): 69–77.

Pedersen, Loren E. *Dark Hearts: The Unconscious Forces that Shape Men's Lives.* Boston and London: Shambhala Publications, 1991.

Quenk, Alex T. *Psychological Types and Psychotherapy.* Gainesville, Fla.: Center for Applications of Psychological Type, 1984.

Quenk, Alex T., and Naomi L. Quenk. "The Use of Psychological Typology in Analysis." In *Jungian Analysis,* edited by Murray Stein. LaSalle, Ill., and London: Open Court, 1982.

Reardon, Agnes. *Personality and Morality: A Developmental Approach.* Woolrich, Me.: TBW Books, 1983.

Rossi, Ernest. "The Cerebral Hemispheres in Analytical Psychology." *Journal of Analytical Psychology* 22 (1977): 32–51.

Sandner, Donald F., and John Beebe. "Psychopathology and Analysis." In *Jungian Analysis,* edited by Murray Stein. LaSalle, Ill., and London: Open Court, 1982.

Sattel, Jack W. "Men, Inexpressiveness, and Power." *Language, Gender, and Society,* edited by Barrie Thorne, Cherris Kramarae, and Nancy Henley. Rowley, Mass.: Newberry House, 1983.

Sharp, Daryl. *Personality Types: Jung's Model of Typology.* Toronto: Inner City Books, 1987.

Spoto, Angelo. *Jung's Typology in Perspective.* Boston: Sigo Press, 1989.

Strongman, Ken. T. *The Psychology of Emotion.* Third ed. New York: John Wiley & Sons, 1987.

Tannen, Deborah. *You Just Don't Understand: Women and Men in Conversation.* New York: Ballantine Books, 1990.

von Franz, Marie-Louise. *C. G. Jung: His Myth in Our Time.* Boston and Ontario: Little, Brown and Co., 1975.

von Franz, Marie-Louise, and James Hillman. *Lectures on Jung's Typology.* Irving, Tex.: Spring Publications, 1971.

Willeford, William. *Feeling, Imagination, and the Self: Transformations of the Mother-Infant Relationship.* Evanston, Ill.: Northwestern University Press, 1987.

———. "The Primacy of Feeling: Part I. Affectivity, the Ego, and the Feeling Function." *Journal of Analytical Psychology* 21 (1976): 115–133.

———. "The Primacy of Feeling: Part II. Relations Among the Functions." *Journal of Analytical Psychology* 22 (1977): 1–16.

Yabroff, William. *The Inner Image: A Resource for Type Development*. Palo Alto, Calif.: Consulting Psychologists Press, 1990.

Yeakley, Flavil R. "Implications of Communication Style Research for Psychological Type Theory." *Research in Psychological Type* 6 (1983): 5–23.

Yeakley, Flavil R. "Communication Style Preferences and Adjustments as an Approach to Studying Effects of Similarity in Psychological Type." *Research in Psychological Type* 5 (1982): 30–48.

Index

Credits